PRAIS

*The Gathering Place* is poignant and thrilling. There were gasp out loud moments and times that made me nod in agreement. Stevens' writing is beautiful. I was constantly taken with the imagery of her words. For instance, *my heart felt like warm melted gold*. I had a deeper understanding of what trauma looks and feels like to a baby and was encouraged in my own healing journey after reading this timeless memoir. You won't be able to put it down!

— REBECCA AUTUMN SANSOM
CREATOR OF THE DOCUMENTARY
*RECKONING WITH THE PRIMAL WOUND*

Why should an adult who had been adopted as an infant be kept in the dark about their origins? Emma Stevens resorts to breaking and entering, tracking down leads like a bloodhound, and getting to the bottom of who she truly is in this powerfully written and compelling autobiography. Emma Stevens has worked hard to not only find out where she came from, but also to heal from the wounds and bewilderment caused by separation. Her beautifully written narrative is a testament to her tenacious and resilient spirit, and an inspiration to adoptees and others seeking answers to the all-important question of life: Who Am I?

— DIANE SHIFFLETT
ADOPTEE

*The Gathering Place* brings you to the center of your heart after first bringing you into the center of the mayhem grief causes to the body and the mind. Emma Stevens has done the hard work—she even broke into a building in order to find pieces of her story—and in doing so and on taking us with her on her journey, we get to benefit from her dedication to the truth, and we learn the repercussions of being adopted and the years and years of work it can take to finally find yourself. And we are inspired: if Emma can find peace and joy, so can we.

— ANNE HEFFRON
AUTHOR AND WRITING COACH,
*YOU DON'T LOOK ADOPTED*

# THE GATHERING PLACE

## AN ADOPTEE'S STORY

## EMMA STEVENS

To Anne,
thanks for the
"win" Coach!
Much love,
Linda

Copyright © 2021 by Emma Stevens

Cover photograph by Ryan Parker, Unsplash Photography

All rights reserved.

No part of this book may be reproduced in any form or by any electronic or mechanical means, including information storage and retrieval systems, without written permission from the author, except for the use of brief quotations in a book review.

This is a work of creative nonfiction. The events are portrayed to the best of Emma Stevens' memory. While all the stories in this book are true, some names and identifying details have been changed to protect the privacy of the people involved.

*For my brother.*
*I wasn't ready to say goodbye.*

# CONTENTS

It matters not how strait the gate,
How charged with punishments the scroll,
I am the master of my fate:
I am the captain of my soul.

— WILLIAM ERNEST HENLEY
"INVICTUS"

# INTRODUCTION

## A CHANGE IS COMING

*Love demands freedom. It always has, and it always will.*

— ROB BELL
AUTHOR *LOVE WINS*,
SPIRITUAL WRITER, HOST OF THE ROBCAST

As I gazed ahead, the late afternoon sun cast a beautiful golden yellow glow over the hills surrounding The Gathering Place. There was just the right amount of shadow making the big old oak tree on top of the main hill look even more majestic than its size already did. My heart raced in anticipation of reaching that spot soon. Hurriedly, I hiked down the hill to start my final climb that would bring me to the foot of the enormous tree. The gentle breeze was warm and smelled sweet with the aroma of the tall green grasses and wildflowers. I eagerly began my ascent on the narrow hard-packed path that wound up the hill to the big tree. Placing the palm of my hand on the rough, thick bark, I felt the warmth of the sun still there. I breathed in deep and closed my eyes and imagined my feet being as firmly planted on the ground as the tree's roots were reaching deep into the earth. I could feel how the trunk was the heart and soul of this tree. And in another way, the skin and bones. My heart felt an openness with a sense of belonging to this place that felt so familiar. Many times, I'd walked here and gazed out over the hills in my dreams. This was to be my gathering place, the safe haven where I had invited everyone on my list to come, enjoy, and relax. A transformative place that would lead to finding the road back to me.

Courage and determination were needed for me to move forward and watch this reunion unfold. It also took much intentionality, focus, and patience to get to this new way of thinking. I was eager to accept the challenges. While it'd taken pain and adversity to welcome this reunion into existence, I was and am wholeheartedly convinced I don't want to waste one more second without honoring this awakening. *Courage don't fail me now.*

I welcomed this change with open arms and was filled with a knowingness that my quest was unconquerable. It felt as important to me as taking my next breath. And that next breath smelled like salvation to me. I had an overwhelming understanding that I could take this journey — *if* I was ready to lay down my heavy cloak of burdens that were never mine to carry in the first place. I had unknowingly and erroneously been led to believe that the actions and behaviors of others were mine alone to own.

My journey involves multiple journeys of overcoming obstacles and "coming out of the fog" in order to find a way HOME. It's the piecing together of all these discoveries that has led me to seeing the need to create a safe, loving, and secure place such as The Gathering Place. There's no breath in living half a life, one that is fear-based and steeped in denial and secrecy.

While none of us can go back and change the past, we do have the ability to reprocess memories and create new pathways in which to experience them in a new healthier way. I've found an effective tool to help me with this transformation. There are many psychotherapeutic methods I could (and) have tried, but I chose Eye Movement Desensitization and Reprocessing (EMDR) for this particular reunion of my parts. The first step was to allow my mind and brain to choose a safe and nurturing place for the work to begin. I selected a welcoming image from my mind's eye and named it — *The Gathering Place.*

While this story may take on a more fantastical sense, and at times seen more through the lens of a child, it is my hard-won liberation narrative.

# FALLING FROM THE SKY

*Our whole life is solving puzzles.*

— Ernő Rubik
Inventor of the Rubik's Cube

I have always been curious and inquisitive. It's both an attribute and a sort of undoing. As a child, when I'd use my curiosity as a tool for deepening my understanding (like learning the art of singing) and a way to be creative, it was an attribute. However, when I'd use it and not realize I was falling down a deep rabbit hole (like disregarding my safety), that usually proved to be more problematic. Ever since I was told by my parents as young as I can remember that my birth mother loved me so much she had to walk away, I've had a difficult time separating fantasy from reality. My inquisitiveness about who my birth mother was became my sole purpose to discover. But until I was old enough to do that, I would fantasize about what she looked like and where she could be.

A good portion of my youth was spent wondering if the

woman I'd just passed on the street might be my birth mother. Or was she that kind woman that helped me at the park last week by giving me a band-aid and a sucker when I'd fallen off the monkey bars? Or — and this was my most recurring fantasy — could she be Samantha, the good witch from the 1960's television show, "Bewitched?" And why not? It could have been her. I thought I looked a lot more like the actress, Elizabeth Montgomery, who portrayed Samantha on the show than I did my adoptive family. Or did I fall aimlessly from the sky? Just free floating down to earth with no history, and with not an inkling of where I was to be going. That's how I've always felt about my beginnings.

I was born on July 21, 1964, in Colorado Springs. My birth mother was 23 years old and resided in the Salvation Army Booth Memorial Home, one of many maternity homes in the early 1960's, until she gave birth. I later learned she took nine days to finally decide to relinquish me. I was in the care of social workers while she was coming to terms with making her final decision, and then remained in their care after she relinquished me.

I often wonder about that little baby, who was me, and how I was processing those early days and months of my life. Social worker notes declare that I was a "sober" baby — watching and observing, but not crying. The notes indicate that I was not interested in eating or smiling. The weight graft chart showed a direct correlation with my birth and my relinquishment date where my weight dropped exponentially. I was most likely in shock and already using my curious nature to figure out my situation. I was placed with my adoptive family approximately 12 weeks after my birth. My adopters had adopted a baby boy from the same agency two and a half years earlier. My parents always told me he was to be the brother that was to be there for me, especially after they were gone. In just three months after being born I had already lost my birth family indefinitely, lost whoever I was under the care of in a foster house, and gained a new mom, dad, and brother.

The Rubik's Cube, originating in the 1970's, is a 3-D combination puzzle with an internal pivot mechanism that enables each face to turn independently, thus mixing up the colors. The goal of the puzzle is to start with some randomized, shuffled, messy configuration of the cube and, by rotating the faces, get back to the original solved pattern with each side being a single color. That's how I've internalized my life from as early as I can remember — like it was an impossible paradox of a puzzle I'd been given, with no instructions, to try and figure out. Fortunately, I've always seemed to have a spirit of tenacity and resilience, which has helped me remain determined and dedicated in trying to problem solve with the information I've been given. Unfortunately, there was not an abundance of information that made a lot of sense.

I knew from early on that my role in the family was to play the part of a dutiful daughter to my parents and little sister to my big brother. My parents implicitly and explicitly taught me that we'd get along better if I conformed to their version of me, and that I understood that no other versions would be tolerated. I wrestled with putting on this impossible mask that didn't fit because it conflicted with who I truly was.

My mother would often say things like, "Emma, go put on that little outfit I bought you. You know, the one with the miniskirt and the little white go-go boots? And you can stand with your back to me and look over your shoulder at the camera." I was five years old at the time and often felt like a puppet for them to show off, someone they could mold and shape to get their own needs met and pretend I came to them as a blank slate. It's as if my parents had requested a dog who would fetch their slippers, instead of the inquisitive cat, who was me. It would take me decades to even come close to solving the impossible Rubik's cube challenge set before me.

# A MAGICAL PORTAL

*The opposite of faith is not doubt; the opposite of faith is control. You must leave the Garden, where there are angels with flaming swords to keep you from ever really returning. You must leave the womb to be born.*

— RICHARD ROHR
AMERICAN AUTHOR, SPIRITUAL WRITER,
AND FRANCISCAN FRIAR

Spending time at The Gathering Place just felt right, like returning home from a long and arduous trip. The light blue sky contrasting with the cumulus clouds, the air smelling sweet, all made me feel safe and full of promise. The expansiveness of the rolling green hills invited me to fill my lungs with all the air that could fit into one intentional inhale. Every slow exhale was a chance to release all preconceived ideas of somehow being in control of anything or anyone but myself. I began to check the surroundings around the tree, the path, and the hill itself to ensure everyone I'd invited to the reunion would feel *safe and feel a sense of home.* I was overcome with a knowingness that they would.

One of the best surprises was the simple rope and wood-seated swing that was hanging from the big old oak tree. It became the magical portal that could lead to another place, time, or emotion. What a wonderful enhancement this was! I quickly inspected the integrity of the old swing, making sure it would support my weight. While I immediately knew which one of my guests would claim the swing, I also knew all the others would want their turn, too. And rightfully so. They've all been together in this story, some earlier and some later, but they've all played their significant integral part.

I sat in the swing and just rested a moment. My feet firmly planted on the soft earth, my hips square in the swing, and my gaze soft and relaxed. As the light breeze began to blow, I allowed my body to begin to sway. Before I knew it, I was playing with lifting one foot off the ground, and then the other. Next, I was slowly swinging in a smooth rhythm that had me leaning back on the assent and leaning forward on the descent. My thoughts wandered to a recent under-standing I'd been contemplating. The idea that life, if we're listening, brings us all to a proverbial fork in the road, if we decide to take the challenge. It's a road where we willingly enter a liminal space to allow for a transformation, or not. It's in that "in-between" space where we learn to let go of our unrealistic expectations and to instead embrace our reality. We find acceptance of all that was, all that is, and of all the possibilities that might come next.

It's thoughts like these that lead me to wonder, isn't it reasonable to think that Adam and Eve were always intended to leave the garden? What if the point is that to become more fully integrated and whole, it means we all must leave the utopia of the garden in order to find perspective? The ques-tion that seems to drive humans is exploring the meaning of our existence and our purpose. I wonder whether I would have searched for meaning as diligently if I'd stayed in such a garden of tranquility. What would have driven me outside the perimeter of a place where I was content, if it weren't for the promise of deeper understanding of self and others? I can reflect on my life now and clearly see that I needed a certain amount of existential angst to allow the tension in my life to pull me forward. And the freewill that I'd been given to explore life was up to me to use either for healthy positive change, or for unhealthy resistance and bondage to the inauthentic.

As I was thinking about my thinking, and seeing my own self swinging on the swing in my mind's eye, I listened to the old, frayed rope of the swing stretch, creak, and almost groan with each sway. I loved swinging on the swings at my elementary school. Sometimes I'd swing slow, as I was then, but other times I became a master full-scale swinger who threatened to tump the set over if I didn't slow it down a bit. When I eventually tired of the sky-high, lean back in the seat, arms stretched long, legs extended to the air mode of swinging, it would be time for the big finale. It was time for my launch out of the swing and into the air! I was fearless in those moments. Most often my ejections from the swing were successful, however, my official first grade school picture clearly shows a large strawberry on the corner of my forehead indicating there was a definite margin of error.

Suddenly aware of how adrift my thoughts were, I attempted to anchor myself back in the present. I needed to prepare myself for what was coming next. At that moment, I only needed to feel the warmth of the sun on my cheeks while waiting patiently to see who my first guest would be to arrive.

# A CHILDHOOD COLORED BY ADOPTION

*Most of the adoptive parents I have seen have never considered that the two most prevalent things operating in their child are grief and fear.*

— NANCY VERRIER
AUTHOR OF *THE PRIMAL WOUND*
AND *COMING HOME TO SELF*

"Since you keep asking about this, it makes me think we're just not good enough for you. Is that it?!" my mom said with her eyes flaming and fists and jaw clenched.

She was irate the few times I dared ask about my adoption story. Because of outbursts like this, I had developed a sense of guilt that made me feel I should apologize for being adopted. It also made me feel apologetic for being me and not who they desired me to be. I adapted my behavior in so many ways to try to feel loved and accepted. This was one of the ongoing results of not being allowed to know my story without condemnation and consequences. So was feeling apologetic for taking up too much space.

"Why would you ask about your birth mother after all

your father and I have done for you? Nothing's ever good enough for you, is it?! I think we should take you to the poor side of town so you can see how grateful you should really be." My mother spoke harshly as she leaned forward, looking as though she was going to lunge at me.

I felt myself shrinking in front of her as she spoke. My body was absorbing the shame and it was being stored in my gut. I immediately regretted voicing curiosity about my birth story. Episodes like this taught me to mask my feelings, especially when the topic was adoption. I don't think I was as concerned about being taken back to the adoption agency as I was fearful of the emotional deprivation that was so often both my parent's style of discipline. They could give me the silent treatment for excruciatingly long periods of time. At least it seemed that way to me as a young child. The way to make them stop was to acquiesce and say that I was very sorry. That's how I became a people pleaser and eventually, a perfectionist. These maladaptive tools gave me a way to keep them relatively happy and keep peace in the family. I also loved them and looked to them for my livelihood. It became clear to me I had to become someone else in order to receive their love and acceptance.

My brother and I were like mismatched bookends. We were both shy children — I'm not sure if this was by nature or by nurture — but Tim made me look like an extrovert in comparison. We lived as brother and sister in the same house for 18 years, but he was a withdrawn little boy that I never really got to know. He was my first attachment that I consciously remember. I looked to him as a possible place of safety and emotional support. However, he was not equipped to provide either of those things for me, or even to himself. When I was about four years old, I became very frightened at nighttime and had it in my mind to escape to the presumed safety and comfort of my brother's room. He would be asleep, and I would very slowly creep into his room and try noiselessly crawling into his creaky bed with him. The slower I went, the louder the mattress springs would squeak. When I'd finally gotten all the way into the bed, my body sweating and my heart racing, only then was I able to fall asleep.

"Emma! What the hell are you doing in your brother's room?! You've been told to stay in your own room! What is *wrong* with you?!" my parents screamed.

"Get back to your room – NOW!"

Shocked awake, I realized I'd forgotten to crawl silently back unseen to my own bed just before sunrise. I had been caught. I felt my body immediately flush with shame, condemnation and embarrassment. After this scenario had happened far too many times, my brother began to resent me coming to his room because he got in trouble too. I can't say that I blamed him. He didn't cause any of the reasons why I was afraid at night. I truly hadn't meant to get him into trouble. I would learn later, when Tim would be the one to get into trouble most often, that it's no fun getting caught in the crosshairs of my parent's wrath and you weren't even responsible for it happening.

One Easter when I was around three years old and my brother was five and a half, he ran into my room crying, "The Easter Bunny! The Easter Bunny! Emma, wake up!" Tim's eyes were wild with excitement. I awoke in my pale-yellow crib wearing my footed pajamas and immediately stood up placing my hands on the top of the rail.

Bouncing up and down in front of my crib, he continued gasping for air, "Hurry! I just saw him! The Easter Bunny! He was here. He's out front!"

Tim stretched upward with his little body to reach over into my crib on his tippy-toes to help me quickly scale the railing. It took a few yanks and pulls to get me over the rail but then we scrambled to our feet. We were running as fast as two young children in their footed pajamas could to chase the bunny and hopefully get another glimpse of him hopping down the road where my brother said he last saw him.

"What'd the bunny look like?!" I asked as I yanked on his pajama sleeve. Tim's exuberance about having seen the bunny was infectious.

"I want to see him too!" I whined as we stood in our pj's together on our front lawn looking down our neighborhood street for signs of a big white hopping bunny.

"I think he's gone now, Emma. He was hopping sooo fast!"

We solemnly turned, slowly walking back to the house to look at the baskets the bunny had left us. We felt special that my brother had seen him, and I had almost gotten to see him. I remember thinking this magical experience was all thanks to my big brother.

In cherished moments such as those, I adored my brother Tim. He had a tender heart at that age, and I wanted nothing more than to hold onto him. I imagine I also looked at him as a possible resource that I could rely on to protect me. I had fantasized that he had superpowers to help me feel loved and cared for. Someone that could help soothe the fear, grief, and pain that I already had inside but didn't even know it. I had no words for, or ways to describe this pain yet.

When Tim went to first grade and was in school full time, I missed him with a relentless longing. Since he wasn't at home with my mom and me during the day as much, I interpreted this as proof that I was not good enough for him to stick around for. My dad was seldom home and not a permanent presence due to his busy work and that often caused him to travel. I had dark feelings of loss that I now understand originated from being severed from my biology at birth. In the book, *The Primal Wound*, author Nancy Verrier names this separation trauma as complex and perplexing, and that this loss affects an adoptee's way of being in the world. My big brother going to first grade activated this original wound of mine. It was exacerbated by Tim suddenly having new school friends his age and him making it painfully clear that I was not a part of his new world. I now see that this is about the time I started feeling drawn to the safety of my brother's room each night. I was trying to soothe my pain over what I perceived as him leaving me. I was missing him so much. Tim, in turn, was pushing me away since he was growing into a new phase of his young life to become more independent, and he was gaining friends his own age. I was crushed and felt that familiar feeling of emotional deprivation that seemed to be a spirit that hung around me. It was a panicky feeling of being afraid that things I loved would always leave me. Whether it be in physical distance or by an emotional separation, it still felt the same.

My relationship with Tim was never the same after our early years. Throughout our lives, our parents played us against each other. I never knew if it was consciously or unconsciously that our parents did this. But the result was that Tim and I did not trust each other. Our parents would say off-hand remarks to me, "Your brother is so smart! He doesn't even have to crack a book to get straight A's!" Then it was, "You should ask your brother for help with that math. I don't want to have to drive you to school early in the morning to get you help from the teacher." I didn't ask Tim for help with my math, and he didn't offer. The fact was, Tim and I did not feel like brother and sister. It just didn't work. He had no brotherly instincts leading him to desire to take care of his little sister. I, in turn, no longer trusted him ever since our very early years where I felt he'd left me. Little did I know, he was fighting his own battle of low self-worth and confusion that made him also want to apologize for taking up too much space.

My happiest childhood memories were mostly at the pool in summertime. I loved the cool water and then getting warmed by the toasty sun. The anticipation I would feel up till the time one of my parents would drive us there was like watching a clock loudly, slowly ticking on the wall. The pool represented happiness to me. I had friends there that taught me the trick of buying a Hershey's chocolate bar with almonds at the snack bar and then letting it slightly melt and get gooey in the sun. It was messy but so good! My brother and I would stay at the pool all day, almost every day. I think my parents used it as a babysitter service for us. The sounds at the pool — splashing water, the squeaky-creaky rebounding sound of someone bouncing off the diving board, the whistle being blown by a lifeguard, sounds of laughter, sounds of people having fun— I loved them all so much! I was fascinated by the diving board and became a good springboard diver. I learned early in life that anything you do in repetition could improve your skill. My tenacity led me to trying to perfect each dive that I learned. I was that kid who waited in line, climbed up onto the diving board, and bounced one too many times, which usually led to the lifeguard blowing his/her whistle for me to go ahead and just dive. And then, after diving in, I would walk/run with my feet slapping the hot, wet concrete right back to getting in line again. I would repeat this process for a good portion of my happy day.

I felt free and energized at the pool. Some of my best friends at the pool were the lifeguards. I felt as if I were their favorite because of them allowing me to climb up their life-guard tower to sit with them. One of them was named Bill. He was kind and protective of me which made me feel safe with him.

"Come on up, Emma!" Bill would shout as he smiled down at me with his deeply tanned face, making his teeth look even whiter. I would crawl right up the lifeguard tower, as agile as a cat. He seemed so old, although looking back, I'm sure he was under 18 years old. I adored the attention and felt special. Maybe I was even feeling as though it was OK to be me and not pretend to be anyone else.

"You've been here a long time again today," Bill said with a concerned look as he jostled my sun-dried messy hair that smelled of chlorine. It was getting close to the time when the pool would be closing for the evening. "Do you know where your parents are? Should I try calling them for you?" I told him they were on the golf course that was right there on the property.

"I can stay until they come," Bill said kindly. "We're trying to get a hold of them now. You just sit tight and I'm sure they'll be here soon." Although I was hungry, I was very happy to be spending extra time with my favorite lifeguard friend who seemed interested in protecting me. I felt very lucky.

Later, as my brother and I sat at the edge with just our feet in the pool, I realized just how hungry I was. Tim and I hadn't eaten since breakfast and by then, it was at least 8:00 p.m. We were under strict orders to never order food from the snack bar since my parents said it was too expensive. After all that swimming, diving, and hot sun, I would start to get bad headaches. Tim, being a redhead, and very fair skinned with a ton of freckles, had a severe sunburn. He was already peeling from a previous burn and was picking at it with his fingernails to remove layers of dead skin. The pool was closed for cleaning by this time, so Tim and I would sit on the front steps at the entrance to the pool waiting patiently for our parents to arrive and take us home.

# MY FIRST GUEST

*Time is change; we measure its passing by how much things alter.*

— Nadine Gordimer
South African writer, political activist,
and recipient of the 1991 Nobel Prize in Literature

At The Gathering Place, I found a comfortable spot to spread my blanket underneath the big old oak tree. I sat down and shut my eyes as I let my mind wander. The warm breeze on my skin felt so relaxing. All I could hear were the birds, the light wind blowing the leaves of the oak tree, and the sound of my breathing. My senses were heightened, and I had the feeling that I was just floating. I focused on letting go of all my tension still left in my forehead, in my jaw, in my cheeks, and everywhere else in my body. This is a meditative exercise that my daily yoga practice has enlightened me to. Hindu philosophy states that the core of every person is not the body, nor the mind, nor the ego, but the soul of the self. The Hindu word "Atman" is the spiritual essence in all creatures, their real innermost essential being.

It is eternal, it is the essence, it is ageless. This philosophy feels true to me, and is often in my daily mantra.

I took a slow inhale into my belly first, feeling it rise. Completing the inhale, I felt my chest rise. I held the breath for five seconds. Then slowly letting my breath out in the opposite direction with a slow exhale from my chest first, and then my belly. As I focused on my breathing, I was imagining inhaling "all things love," and exhaling "letting things go." The reason I was there at The Gathering Place was to let some things go. Things that no longer served me and were not needed in my life anymore. I felt that I was more than ready to lay these things down that were hindering me to be my true self. I was hoping that the guests I'd invited would be coming to help me do just that.

Without even opening my eyes, I could sense that the late afternoon sun was shifting, and the breeze was becoming faintly cooler. Still relaxed, I became aware of a faint voice in the distance. The sound was getting closer, and I thought it might be – but I wasn't sure – a small child singing? Now I could feel my present self very much in the here and now. I felt the weight of my body sitting on the ground under the big old oak tree, and my eyes were wide open and alert. Slowly focusing, I saw her. My first guest. The waters of my soul were stirring by seeing her approach. I could hear her sweet voice singing a melodic tune, and saw she was wearing a white eyelet flowing dress with a pink ribbon that held back her long light brown hair. The little one I'd invited, who was five years old, was singing and gathering wildflowers as she bravely walked up the narrow hard-packed dirt path to meet me under the big old oak tree.

# THE CROSSWALK GAME

*Until you make the unconscious conscious, it will direct your life and you will call it fate.*

— CARL JUNG
SWISS PSYCHIATRIST

I adored my first grade teacher, Mrs. Sanders. She was a kind and loving grandmotherly type. I liked my school and I liked being with other children and learning new things. I lived on the same side of the street as the school and could walk through the neighborhood to get there and home with my brother. One day, something very interesting caught my eye. It was a woman wearing a yellow and orange vest carrying a hand-held stop sign. As I watched her, it looked like she was caring for a group of children from my school. They gathered close around her as she bent to their height looking as if she might be telling them a secret. Still watching, I saw the woman in the brightly colored vest hold the stop sign up high and gesture for the street traffic to halt. I had then learned that this designated spot was called a crosswalk identified by the painted white lines on the street.

EMMA STEVENS

I also learned that the crossing guard's duty was to walk the children safely across the street while the cars would patiently wait. My curiosity piqued, I started to watch every day as the kindly woman guard would do this for the children who lived across the street from the school. It looked fun to me! It looked like the woman really cared for these children's safety and wellbeing. I devised a plan to see whether I could be part of what seemed like a very fun game.

"Well, hello there! What's your name? Are you new to our school?" The nice lady crossing guard asked me. My six-year-old self didn't know how to answer, so I just leaned in closer to her and tried to blend in with the other kids.

My heart pounded with anticipation since the guard was already preparing to stop the traffic so we could safely cross the street. I closely observed what the other kids were doing and tried to do the same. The last thing I wanted was to act like I didn't belong to this crosswalk group and be called out as an imposter. Maybe the kind guard would have a know-ingness of who her chosen dear ones were and if I didn't act appropriately, she would swiftly exclude me from her deserving ones.

And then, just like a waddling of ducklings, we were walking. The momentum of the group carried me across the temporary safe zone that the kind woman had created as if I were floating in a pink bubble. This guard seemed to have the power and authority to make the whole world stop in order to love, protect and serve us. The excitement and novelty of it all had me in a state of euphoria and gave me a sense that I was alive. To this crossing guard, I was deemed lovable and important enough to keep safe. These were some realities that deep down I knew I was missing and desper-ately needed to find, if only for a moment.

"OK, kids! Have a nice afternoon!" The crossing guard

waved goodbye to us all as she started back towards the school side of the street.

"Bye! Thank you! See you tomorrow!" We all cheerfully called to her. It seemed to me that the experience that I craved to be a part of was over in a matter of minutes.

After being at school all day, most kids, including myself, felt elation over the day being over. Now that we were across the street from where we'd spent the whole day in a structured mode, we were now free to talk, run and laugh out loud as much as we wanted. As I moved along with the other kids, they started going their separate ways, one by one. It was at that moment I realized I was standing alone in a neighborhood that was not my own, without a clue of what to do next. The houses were different. The streets were different. Even my familiar school across the street looked different since I was seeing it from a very different perspective. I closed my eyes and felt the pounding of my heart in my ears and a feeling of growing shame and embarrassment that I looked like someone who didn't have a clue of what they were doing, or where they were going.

Fear and shame kept me from flagging down the crossing guard and confessing to her of my folly. Now my excited feeling had turned into total panic. Panic of how to get back across the street without letting anyone know what I'd done. I was afraid the guard would be mad at me for wasting her time and using her service which I didn't even need. I'd also be admitting that I indeed didn't belong to her special group of children that she seemed devoted to love and protect. My own mother would be furious and telling me how ridiculous I'd been to "pull such a stunt." I walked farther down the street from where the guard had safely delivered us and made sure she couldn't see me. Internally, my anxiety was churning, and my fear had spiked my heartrate to the point where my arms and legs were shaking uncontrollably. I tried watching to see if the coast was clear, but it was difficult since the parallel parked cars along the side of the street were blocking my view. The best I could do was to watch the tops of cars from over the parked cars as they were driving past. There was a popular sci-fi television show at that time called "Land of the Giants." The main characters were tiny and would often try escaping from being stepped on and crushed by the giants who could be people or insects or other dangers. I felt as though that was me in that moment being so small and trying to survive in a world much larger. Alone and very scared, my strategy (if it could be called that) to get back across the street was to make a run for it. I rationalized that not getting caught was more important than my safety. So, I crossed my fingers, closed my eyes, and hoped to not get hit by any moving cars.

I remember thinking, as I darted out into the street between two parked cars, *I know I'm going to get hit*. And then I did. The young woman driving the car that struck me was thankfully traveling the school speed zone limit of 25 miles per hour. But even at that speed, when the front bumper of her car hit my upper body, it launched me approximately 20 to 25 feet up the road. Luckily, I had a big, fluffy, winter coat on that day that helped buffer my body from the damaging impact of skidding and circling on the pavement all that way on my back. I remember lying motionless looking up at the sky after finally coming to a full stop. The world went completely silent as I experienced a sleepy floaty feeling and tried to identify what the damage to my body was as I lay in the middle of the street.

"Oh, my dear, dear, just lie still. Help is on the way. I'm right here with you." I heard a woman speaking to me kindly as she placed her coat on top of me and tucked it in around my body. I was so cold, probably feeling the effects of being in shock. She seemed like an angel to me as I was in a semiconscious state. She was soothing me, quietly talking to me, and keeping me warm the best she could. It's as if she sensed just how much I needed her compassion and her calmness in those moments. I vividly remember thinking, "I wonder if this woman is my birth mother. She's being so very nice to me! Could it be her?!" I wondered. I softened at her touch and was feeling regulated by her just being there beside me and caring for me.

"Emma, I'm coming!" I suddenly heard the frantic calls of my mom as she rushed up alongside us. Someone in the neighborhood must have told her to come quickly, so she ran to the scene of the accident as fast as she could. Her first words were, "What in the world were you thinking!" Holding her head in both of her hands she cried out, *"You've been hit by a car! Oh my God, you've been hit by a car!"*

"I'm OK, mom. I'm not going to die." I said weakly, trying to reassure and console her. Speaking just these few words took so much effort. It felt as though I was hearing my voice coming from down a very long dark tunnel. Since I was more concerned with how she felt than with my own current dire situation, I tried to appear in a much better state than I truly was. My concern also shifted to how much trouble I was more than likely going to be in. That old familiar anxiety in my stomach had begun and was followed by feelings of impending doom. By then, I had lost track of the nice woman that had generously given me her coat and had stayed with me making me feel not so afraid and alone. I was very sad she wasn't there anymore.

I had a broken left collar bone and was sent home from the hospital with an awkward brace I was to wear for months. The brace was shaped much like an infinity symbol with two loops in which to slip on like a little coat. It was designed to help hold my shoulder blades together in the back like a safety pin and keep my chest open, and shoulders back. One good thing the broken left collarbone provided was that it became my new way of learning how to distinguish my left from my right. The end of the left clavicle by my throat poked out just a bit now, and I would absently thump it and know that it was my left side. The peculiar thing to me was that no one ever asked me what I was doing by going across the street with the crosswalk. If anyone thought it was strange that I ended up across a street I didn't need to cross, they didn't say anything. In hindsight, another missed opportunity to help a young girl sort some important things through. There were some deep truths about why I felt drawn to not only wanting to be a part of the crosswalk game, but how drawn I was to the crossing guard who looked like love and security to me. She represented a sense of belonging and connectedness to something I wanted so badly and that I was willing to risk my safety. This similar scenario would play itself out more than once in my life where I was hopeful to find my birth mother in almost any stranger I met who was kind to me.

# THE LITTLE GIRL WITH THE LIGHT BROWN HAIR

*Sawubona: All my attention is with you. I see you and I allow myself to discover your needs, to see your fears, to identify your mistakes and accept them. I accept you for what you are and you are part of me.*

— A ZULU GREETING

This amazing little girl had journeyed to meet me under the big old oak tree on the hill at The Gathering Place. "Hey, look what I can do! Do you want to see what I can do?!" She said these words with infinite joy and a big infectious smile. Without waiting a split second for my response, she proceeded to do her version of a cartwheel, again, and again. I excitedly applauded her as I felt my own joy rise just watching her.

Giggling, she said, "My name is Tabitha. What's yours?" Her non-stop cartwheels continued in a haphazard but charming succession.

I remembered this age so well. Full of energy and spirit. I was so eager to have fun, but I also felt emotions deeply. I once sobbed uncontrollably at a Disney movie called *The*

*Incredible Journey* about two dogs and a cat being separated from their home and owners, that my mom almost made us leave early. She took me to the bathroom trying to calm me down and to ask me why I was so distraught. I now clearly see that the movie had triggered my implicit memories of the original wound and trauma of my own separation from first family and home. All I could verbalize to my mom was to say that it was so sad. I had no language to be able to adequately share with her the deep sadness and sense of hopelessness I was feeling. In other words, I didn't have language to express what had already been stored in my bones.

Another incidence of a seemingly unexplained sadness was when I was around that same age and had a similar reaction to a song released in 1968 titled "Honey, I Miss You" by Bobby Goldsboro. The song tells a story of the happiness and sorrow of a man who loves and cherishes his mate deeply, and then loses her. I would listen to the 45-inch record on my little record player over, and over. The sad but beautiful sound of the violins and the storytelling lyrics evoked in me my first understanding of the meaning of *bittersweet*. When I was told that the woman in the song had died, I cried many tears of knowingness.

"Guess what?" an out-of-breath Tabitha asked. She continued with a few more cartwheels until she came right up alongside of me, "My mommy told me I didn't grow in her tummy. Neither did my big brother. I grew in some other mommy's tummy." She seemed to be speaking to me, but it felt as if she were looking right past me into the distance.

"How does that make you feel?" I really wanted to know. This little one's honesty was enough to make me feel just a little off balance.

"Sad, I guess. I wish I could tell my 'other' mommy I'm OK and tell her where I am. She must be sad, too – not knowing where I am. I don't want her to think I'm lost in the woods – or that the boogie man under my bed got me!"

Tabitha lowered her head then, as if she were about to state an admission of guilt. "That's why I go to my big brother's room at night cuz he's safe. I'm afraid of the monsters under my bed and in my closet." She shivered a moment and continued, "He's gone a lot at school now so that's why I go see him at night. I know I'm bad and it makes mommy and daddy and my brother really mad when I do that. I wish I could write "other" mommy a letter, but mommy gets very mad when I talk about her. She says they saved me cuz I was having a sad life and they were gonna make everything OK now. She said that she and daddy were good people who wanted me. My other mommy had to leave me cuz she couldn't take care of me."

And just then, she brightened and added, "I love my brother — he's in first grade. What's your favorite color? Mine's lellow!"

"Do you miss her?" I moved forward with my questions since it seemed Tabitha was feeling safe and communicative.

"Yeah, I do, I do. It makes me feel like crying, I miss her so much." And then Tabitha concluded, "Now...why didn't she want me?" She raised her gaze to look me in the eyes, and I was both shattered and enchanted by this moment of honesty and clarity. Something inside me, however, told me to be patient. I would answer her question, but I felt the moment was not this one.

Momentarily stunned by her forthrightness, I took a deep breath while gathering my thoughts and said, "Do you have a pet, Tabitha?"

Her face immediately brightened, and her eyes twinkled, "Yes! Her name is Tabby!" At the thought of her beloved cat, Tabitha was back and all aglow.

The sun was getting much lower now. The long casting

shadows were gone and the air much cooler. It would be dark soon. "Can you come see me again tomorrow? I'd love to hear more about you and Tabby."

"How 'bout I bring Tabby with me?! Ooooo! I can't wait! I'm going to dress her up in a dress for you! I do it all the time. She likes it." Tabitha announced. She then turned and scooped up the bunch of wildflowers she had gingerly placed on the ground for safe keeping while she'd been performing her cartwheels.

"Until tomorrow then. It was so nice to meet you, Tabitha."

My heart felt like warm melted gold. The last thing I wanted was to part with her just then, but I knew tomorrow would come and we'd share much more. She turned to go with a big wave goodbye, her light brown ponytail blowing in the breeze, and then skipped down the narrow dirt path that led her to follow the gentle descent of the grassy hill.

# MAPS CARVED IN STONE ARE PROBLEMATIC AT BEST

*Trauma is perhaps the most avoided, ignored, belittled, denied, misunderstood, and untreated cause of human suffering.*

— PETER LEVINE

PSYCHOTHERAPIST, AUTHOR,

AND CREATOR OF SOMATIC EXPERIENCING

Life at home became more difficult to navigate the older my brother and I got. Our pre-teen and teenage years were especially difficult. Mom and dad's priorities seemed to be misplaced and concentrated on things other than raising their children in a happy home in which to thrive. I'm convinced that as a toddler of 18 months old, the reason I was in critical condition suffering from dehydration in the hospital was the result of my unhappiness with my situation. It was as if I'd given up hope of my birth mother ever return-ing. It's also not hard to imagine that the culmination of all those days, months, and then over a year of feeling like I was with strangers in a strange place, were not taking a toll on me. A place that was not home. It didn't feel right, it didn't look right, it didn't smell right, nor did it sound right when I'd be told I was the "light of their lives." I would often be so confused by these conflicting messages of hearing that they loved us, yet they would sit us at the kitchen table berating us for hours. This happened almost nightly where they would vent their frustrations out on us over just about anything. It could've been caused by my dad being late for dinner, or my brother being in trouble for not keeping his room clean, or one of us just looking at them wrong. It really didn't matter. Pouring daily alcohol into the situation in no way helped matters go more smoothly.

My brother and I were held against our will in our respective places at the dark hardwood kitchen table, our heads and shoulders slumped over crying without hope that the abuse would stop anytime soon. The physical, verbal, and mental abuse made me feel gutted and hollowed out. It was heavy and too much to bear. Dissociating was my method of trying to keep safe. As I cried to the extent that my face was puffy — yet tight and dry from the salty tears, I vividly remember telling the different parts of myself that made up the totality of who I was, to float away to safety. I told them to leave, and I would come back and get them when I thought it was safe to do so. But the thing about on-going, repetitive abuse, is that it changes you. It changes your brain. Only years later did I remember my thoughts that I had at that dark hardwood kitchen table. The memory of my promise to myself, to all my parts, to reunite one day for healing and restoration.

I don't know why my brother had less resilience than I seemed to have had to survive our youth. His life was riddled with substance abuse and he generally took very poor care of himself. He had five children and wrestled with the fact that one of his sons developed his own drug addiction problems. My brother didn't have the awareness or insight to handle his son's addictions and risky lifestyle in any other way than being excessively codependent. Tim never saw the need to do his own interior work so as not to pass on and inflict his own son with toxic attitudes and behaviors. This chronic situation with his adult son added to my brother's overall anxiety and it also triggered his unaddressed and unresolved adverse childhood experiences. Subsequently, a life permeated with stress, grief, and trauma became like a choke hold on my brother.

Tim died of a heart attack the year he had barely turned 60. I still grieve the loss of my brother. Today and as long ago as when I was just a small girl who idolized him. The brother who had run into my room that long ago Easter morning when we were so very young telling me he'd just seen the Easter Bunny. I regret not ever telling him how much sadness it brought me to see him across the dark hardwood table crying, just as I was. We were prisoners together during those years of our parents demanding we be who they wanted us to be; to change the very core of who we were. I wish I could have told Tim that it was wrong of our father to tell him he was weak just because he didn't like sports or didn't fit the idea of a man that my father demanded he be. It was heartbreaking, and all I could do was watch. Watch and listen as they berated us both. My method was to dissociate. My brother, Tim, I truly feel, symbolically died at that dark hardwood table.

I recently dreamed I was among thousands of children who were all adoptees and were sleeping in their twin size beds. As far as I could see, there were beds that were veiled by the heavy early misty dawn. I began to float high above them all when I saw some of the children, one out of about every 10, waking up and climbing out of their beds. I also noticed that my brother, Tim, was in the bed right next to mine. He appeared to be in a deep, undisturbed sleep. The ones that were waking up, started looking curiously at each other. And in the silence, there was a growing knowingness that seemed to be dawning on them. A beautiful transformation was taking place but not without the suffering that change always seems to bring.

This gradual awareness was revealing to the awakened adoptees the deeper, fuller meaning of how being adopted had affected them. The loss that includes having no genetic mirroring, loss of generational lineage, loss of culture, feelings of "otherness," deep feelings of grief, lacking continuity of having "the full picture" of their story, loss of safety and trust, loss of control, loss of worth — are but just a few. It was becoming clearer to the awakened adoptees that there was a need to have a kind of death of the previous ways of thinking before there could be a rebirth.

Through patience and grace, they were growing in the knowledge that there was much more to explore and discover before claiming their full coherent and cohesive narrative. In my dream, I tried to awaken my brother in hopes he could heal from his own feelings of loss and grief. However, nothing seemed to disturb him from being peacefully sound asleep. I was silently willing him to open his eyes and be part of this new, more non-dualistic way in which to view life. I desperately wanted Tim to either fight, struggle, or scream – whatever it would take to ensure that he woke up to reclaim himself as these other adoptees were.

It starts for many of us who were adopted soon after their birth, with the rupture caused by being relinquished, being pulled by the root and separated from our birth mothers. Then adapting to a foster home/house where the social workers are usually told not to bond with the child, and then taken to yet another place of their new adoptive home. My adoptive parents had never resolved their issues of infertility and had looked at adoption as their Plan B — a substitute for the real thing. My brother and I were purchased to fill in their perfectly designed family drama about a mommy, daddy, son, and daughter.

My mom had no motherly instincts, no motherly feel about her at all. My brother and I knew she didn't, and I think deep down, she knew it, too. The real tragedy was that she wasn't ever motivated to even try to learn. My mother would often repeat how my brother would cry and arch his back in her arms as an infant. She would tell the story as if there was something wrong with *him*. Seeing through her lens of reality, it was my brother's responsibility and duty to "attune and attach" to her. It's as if she labeled him unlovable from the beginning because she perceived his crying as a rejection of her. I think it was easier for her to blame the baby and deem him ungrateful, than for her to think she may have not been providing my brother with the soothing that he so badly needed.

So many adaptations had to take place for me to survive my childhood. I had gotten so far away from my true self, that later in life when I thought I could return to that truer state of being, I'd forgotten what or who that even was. I learned how to be a perfectionist and erroneously thought this would prevent any problem to be found in me. I now realize that thinking that way brings its own kind of pain. But I would say that this adaptation did keep me more out of harm's way than my brother had been able to do. He seemed to always get caught and was in trouble for most of his youth.

Another of my adaptations was becoming a people pleaser. Since I really had no voice and was silenced harshly whenever I tried to speak my mind, I saw my only choice was to be as pleasing as necessary. In that same vein, I learned to take on and feel responsible for everyone's emotions in my family. If my parents were upset I thought it must be my fault. If my mother cried, saying that my brother and I didn't love her and that we were selfish and ungrateful, I became more determined to be perfect and pleasing. I had long since learned that if I didn't do all these things, I'd undoubtedly be placing myself in danger of facing the repercussions of yet another of their emotional outbursts that I felt at a loss to understand or know how to navigate.

# IN SEARCH OF ME

*This above all: to thine own self be true, And it must follow, as the night the day, Thou canst not then be false to any man.*

— William Shakespeare
English playwright, poet, and actor

My search for my beginnings began in 1985. I was searching for me, not for my birth parents, or birth family. Many years later I would discover that while I was searching for my birth parents, I was still very much in the fog of the totality of how being adopted had colored my life. It would take me decades to discover certain truths to be able to gain that kind of awareness. My mother had always said to me in a disapproving voice, "You're just the kind of person who will probably go searching for your roots." I wanted to say, "And that's a *bad* thing? An *abnormal* thing?" The truth was that I am just that kind of person who is curious about their origins. Me and most everyone else who has lived on the planet. I needed to know my story and have a narrative to be able to understand myself in a real way. In a way that

I'd never been allowed to do as a child. Now that I was 23 years old, I was determined to begin my search in earnest. I had been bending to the will of others all my life. And while I felt empowered to take this journey, I still did it without my family knowing about any of my search. Years later they would find out from my mother's sister who betrayed my confidence and told them my secret. My adoptive parents didn't speak to me for three years and told me that I was disinherited. It was a big price I had to pay for choosing me for the first time in my life.

My search was an amazing time in my life for many reasons. I discovered a strength I never knew I had. A big dose of tenacity and a new sense of confidence led me clue by clue to eventually finding both of my birth parents. Each night after work, I'd be dedicated to working many hours of writing letters, making phone calls, and doing whatever was necessary to keep the ball rolling to gather more and more facts about my adoption. One weekend, when my parents were out of town and I was house sitting for them, I found my adoption decree in the vault. It didn't tell me anything other than learning my birth name, which was very generic. But still, I felt that it was such a discovery. An intimate discovery of learning that I had been named Baby Girl Ridgefort at birth. I now knew something that my birth mother also knew because she had created it. My birth name.

Looking back, I'm not sure how I accomplished what I did without the help or aid of the internet, cell phones, and social media. Instead, I wrote letter after letter, placed phone call after phone call, just hoping others would provide me with the information that would help me figure out yet another piece to my puzzle.

At one point I was so desperate to find a breakthrough clue that I called a nighttime television show that had a psychic reader who took questions on-air. Yes, I really did that. I'll always remember that the host of the show was named, "Desiree." I called the phone number that was posted on-screen, pausing on the last number before finally having the courage to let the call go through. It was busy! I obsessively kept trying and finally heard the phone's dialing tone. My heart racing, I didn't have to wait long before I was speaking to no other than the psychic named Desiree. I nervously formed the words to ask this stranger the most intimate and personal question of my life. All of this on a Friday night television show! She informed me that, "Yes, you will meet your birth mother. And it will be very soon." I took that as a good sign. My insides were quaking so uncontrollably, I couldn't watch the show at the same time of also being the caller. My senses were on overload, and it was difficult to think clearly or ask an understandable question. Her answer to me was like medicine to my soul though. It never occurred to me that she maybe didn't even know what she was talking about when she answered in the affirmative that I would indeed meet my birth mom. Or, when she replied that I would be meeting her very soon. She told me just what I wanted to hear.

I soon tired of just calling the city of my birth and where my adoption took place and decided to make the 10-hour trip there so I could meet one-on-one with an adoption agency representative.

"You're not going to believe this, but I was actually the person who counseled your birth mother and was assigned to her case 24 years ago. I noticed this when I looked at her file," the adoption worker replied.

My skin prickled knowing she had seen my birth mother in person and had actually been involved with the decision that changed the trajectory of my life. I wanted to firmly convey to this agency employee that the *"file"* she so nonchalantly held in her hands was much more than a casual business transaction to me!

And then, it was as if she dropped a bomb on me. She handed me a letter saying it'd been written to the agency by my birth mother.

*"What?!"* I said feeling a surge of adrenaline. It was like a moment in time that was so heavy, it had to come to an abrupt halt. It was then I realized I'd stopped breathing.

"Yes, she wrote to us after she relinquished you." The woman delivered this information as if she were informing me of the current weather forecast. Infuriated, I imagined crawling across the desk to look her square in the eyes and grab her by the shoulders. This worker clearly did not get the depth of what it meant to learn my birth mother had written any kind of message to me, or about me. I couldn't help but compare how her words sounded just the same as if she were telling me "Lunch will be served in the cafeteria today from noon until 2:00 p.m."

The worker went on, "Right after your birth, she surprised us by saying she was now unsure of her decision to relinquish. However, after a week she made her final decision — a loving decision — a selfless act to give you a better life."

I managed to keep my anger to myself thinking of the dysfunctional adoptive home where I had been placed. Hmmm ... it was a different life, for sure. But I'm not convinced a "better" one.

"I think she wrote this note as a loving gesture to say goodbye... and for her to have closure," the woman said.

Several years earlier, when I had started my search in earnest, I began with paying for non-identifying information about my birth family. It struck me as I was sitting across from this adoption worker, that the agency had never sent the body of this letter to me before. And why not?! I felt my temperature rising as my cheeks were getting hot with anger at the realization that this letter could have soothed me long before this. And hadn't I paid a good price for that information? Information that was mine and I felt should be mine alone. And then for the agency to have left out this important letter, of all things. The rest of the non-identifying information I received were things like eye and hair color, number of siblings, occupation at time of my birth, and level of education. None of these non-identifying items helped me in any significant way, and certainly not in providing me with a sense of any emotional wellbeing. And that's not to mention important, maybe even vital information about my family medical history? None of that was given to me, not even for a price.

I stared at the typewritten letter from my birth mother that consisted of approximately a half page of words. The letter was to the attention of the agency worker, and it also contained her well wishes for me. Her wishes were that I have a life she could not have given me. The worker then informed me that they had blacked out my birth mother's name when they made me a copy.

"Many young mothers used fictitious names during their stay at the maternity homes. Your mother did too. So, when she sent this letter to us after she relinquished you, this was the first time we discovered what her true name was."

*This was the first time we discovered what her true name was.* These words kept reverberating inside my head like the deep gong sound of a loud bell.

It was at this point, I started imagining a kind of movie where the agency worker would stand up, my adoption file still wide open on her desk, and she'd announce she had to step out of the room for a moment but would be right back. And it would be at that precise time where I'd be able to quickly look at the file (my file!) in order to jot down my birth mother's real name. But none of that had transpired in this real-life scenario. The meeting ended there with me just having more questions to my questions.

To this day, I'm unsure how moved, or majorly underwhelmed I am regarding the letter my first mom wrote to the adoption agency back in 1964, a few weeks after my birth. It wasn't even specifically written to *me*. I felt the sentiment of her words at first, since they were the only words of hers I'd ever read. However, in a short amount of time, the letter started to take on a slightly more removed and impersonal feel. In all actuality, the worker had phrased it best; the letter's intent was to be *her* closure. A kind of absolving of guilt that would allow her to justify allowing strangers to raise her baby and feel assured that "they" would be a safer place for her baby to land. It would have warmed my heart more if she'd written me a personal note that was to be given to me. And maybe without requiring me to drive 10 hours, only to discover that it'd been there waiting for me - whenever - or maybe never. This is the body of the letter from my birth mother that I received that day while at the adoption agency:

August 1964

I understand the court will give you the complete report of my decision. I suppose I have known all along it would be wrong to keep my baby from having a normal home environment and two parents who love her. Through strength from God I am leaving her behind for you to find a good home for.

Please find a wonderful home where they will love and bring her up to be everything I had hoped she would be. A child has no past only a future and I pray hers will hold everything wonderful.

I just wish I could help her if she ever gets hurt in some way because we never seem to escape life without getting hurt in some way. I wish, too, she would someday realize how much I loved her and wanted her and didn't want to give her up. God will let her know.

Let God guide your hand in selecting a home.

(Name blacked out)

I had accomplished more than I even knew from this visit, though. It finally dawned on me during the long 10-hour drive home that with all the best sleuthing I could manage, it wouldn't ever be enough to find what I was searching for. This was all because my birth mother used a fictitious name on all the documents during her pregnancy. I had already tried in vain to send off for my unamended birth certificate in hopes that someone at Vital Statistics would make a mistake and send me what I felt was mine to have in the first place. Then I had to consider that my birth mom had most likely used a fictitious name even on my birth certificate, as well. Vital Statistics only sent me a cryptic letter of refusal, as if I'd asked for important top-secret information that required a much higher level of clearance than I had. It began to settle on me that the only avenue available to me ever finding my birth parents would be if I could obtain my adoption file from the agency where I had just visited. I needed the file that they possessed that had the letter from my birth mom where she had signed her true name, for the first time since her pregnancy. Realizing this felt as though I had just made some progress on my Rubik's Cube. My curious and tenacious traits were fully activated, and I began to create a plan to make the unknown — known.

# GRACE, A CAT NAMED TABBY, AND SEEING SHADES OF GRAY

*Trauma is not what happens to you. Trauma is what happens inside you, as a result of what happens to you.*

— GABOR MATÉ
HUNGARIAN-CANADIAN PHYSICIAN, AUTHOR,
LECTURER, CHILDHOOD DEVELOPMENT AND TRAUMA

Dreams of Tabitha filled my consciousness since our last meeting at The Gathering Place. I couldn't help thinking of the things that I would be sharing with her during our next visit. I was going to attempt to answer the questions that she'd asked of me. Questions I knew were so important to the essence of who she was and who she'd become. Just looking at her in all her innocence and childlike joy made me sink into my heart. I knew I owed her the truth. Anything other than honesty would just perpetuate the secrets that can be insidious in our lives. The secrets that riddle our lives with falsities and disconnect us from things that are true.

I again found myself waiting patiently for her under the

big old oak tree as I sat looking out over the fields of green and gold. This was my secret place of peace. A place for transformation and reunification of a wide spectrum of all that is, and all that should have been. Fully accepting one's reality is not a feat for those unwilling or unprepared. For many, it takes that "thing," whatever it may be, that brings us to our knees. That thing that we either admit to ourselves that we are powerless over, or we keep flailing in an insane attempt to stay in some false sense of control.

What I can now see was my own blessed downfall and coming to the end of myself was alcoholism. My relationship with alcohol was formed and grounded both through my family's preoccupation with drinking and society's romanticizing of alcohol as a necessity for almost every life event. The message all around me was to use alcohol and that its consumption was normal and necessary to fit in. In fact, not drinking didn't even feel like an option. My first black-out drunk happened on the last day of my seventh grade school year. My friends and I were having a sleep over at a friend's house who had airplane bottles filled with different kinds of alcohol. The bottles were so small. We didn't think they could possibly get us as drunk as they did. I didn't even know what a black-out was. I paid severely for thinking those small bottles were nothing to be afraid of. In fact, they caused me to become violently ill due to mixing many different types of alcohol.

Drinking was part of my life for decades thereafter. My relationship with alcohol didn't always cause me the problems it had that night at the end of seventh grade, but I can see now that it was just biding its time until fully dominating me. The drug was so insidious; I didn't see the take over right away. And then when I did recognize it – it was too late. Alcohol had seized control, manipulating me into thinking it was my best friend, my lover, and that I could not exist without it.

My addiction to alcohol was one thing, but I also came to discover that I had many more "isms" yet to uncover and to be revealed. My existential angst had become so great that I was either going to die, or I was going to find something to grab on to. I had a choice of either staying in the muck, or to unravel and begin anew. I did a little of both, the truth be told. In my early 50's, my structure had thankfully, completely, and mercifully crumbled. It took many therapy hours, Alcoholics Anonymous meetings, many hard looks in the mirror, and a steadfastness that was fueled by continuously staying connected to my source, my spirit, to begin my journey of recovery. A well trusted counselor, Don, acted as my guide out of that dark space and time. He represented a secure attachment, and it was through this stable relationship (that continues present day) that I've learned what healthy attachment looks like.

And then slowly, my dark days started to turn into what the Alcoholic Anonymous big blue book calls having a "spiritual awakening" and "living in the solution." I came to learn that this means trying to live an authentic life. A life trying to stay aligned to your own principles and monitoring your own part in all situations. Befriending your inner child and practicing self-love is also mandatory in beginning to live in this way of grace. I painstakingly and intentionally made the decision to be among the wise who have learned how to carry their burden with grace. As my recovery gained momentum, I started having fireworks of insights that helped me obtain deeper degrees of clarity. I began to have curiosity of how trauma can be a great teacher, if we choose to be brave enough to listen. Many have made these discoveries concerning their own lives, and I will always be grateful for somehow being able to find it for my life, too.

Out in the near distance, little Tabitha began to come into view. My heart was so full to see her making her way back to me yet again. Then I noticed she was not alone. She was pulling a Red Flyer wagon behind her. I couldn't yet make out what it was, but there appeared to be something small in the bed of the wagon.

"It's me! It's me!" she rang out in her sing-song voice. "Look who I bot! It's Miss Tabby Cat!" She stopped her travel long enough to scoop her cat up in her small arms and held her loved pet close. It was then I noticed that Miss Tabby Cat was indeed wearing a pink and yellow flowered doll's dress, just as Tabitha had promised she would dress her for the occasion. It struck me how Miss Tabby was almost larger than little Tabitha. Nevertheless, it was clear that the love she had for this pet was bigger than the two of them put together.

I had the blanket spread out under our tree again and we all settled into a kind of comfortable cozy picnic. I had made sure to bring some treats with me this time. Nothing fancy, just some strawberries, chocolate chip cookies, and lemonade.

"I *wuuv* cookies!" she declared.

"Does Miss Tabby Cat enjoy cat treats?" Tabitha smiled and enthusiastically nodded her head multiple times with a big yes. Tabby seemed intrigued by my offering and showed her approval by a masterful swish-swish of her long fluffy tail, and a blink-blink of her clever and curious golden amber eyes.

"I'm so happy to see you again, Tabitha," I said smiling and taking an opportunity to stroke Tabby's long soft brown and black fur as she sat in the position of a bread loaf. She sat between us, as if she were knowingly acting as a link coupling Tabitha and myself. The funny thing about cats is that they can seem at home in almost any place they dwell.

When they're feeling safe and comfortable, they take a sense of ownership and know their right to take up space. I remembered those eyes of hers, of course. My sweet, adorable Tabby from long ago. She was my first friend, and she had been so very good to me. Tabitha may or may not have realized what a gift she had given me by not only bringing herself here, but our beautiful pet, Tabby, too.

Tabby was my seventh birthday present. My mom asked me to open our pantry door where my present was sitting perched on a shelf just staring out at me from the dim light. I squealed with delight. I hugged my present so tight as if I was never going to let go. "What will you name her?" my mom asked. After learning that she was something called a "Tabby" cat, a domestic cat with a distinctive "M" shaped marking on the forehead, I thought it very original to call her by that same name. *"Tabby!"* I exclaimed.

Tabby was incredibly affectionate and intelligent. We fell in love instantly. She proved to be the best friend of my childhood, by far. It was she who would teach me how to love and how to be loved. She also taught me about companionship, responsibility, loyalty, trust, and how to play. The reciprocity we shared with taking care of one another was nurturing and kind. In my youth, I had mononucleosis in both first and second grade, which left me bed ridden for approximately six weeks each time. Alone and in my room, I would spend endless hours with my friend, Tabby. We often played together in my closet where I had a Crissy doll whose hair could be made to grow, and more often than that, I spent a lot of time dressing Tabby up in my doll dresses. She was always such a great sport about it, too! I would reward her for allowing me to fit her into tight fitting clothing by placing her in an old hat box of my mom's and pulling her around the room. She loved that.

Tabitha was leaning back, supporting herself with her

arms straight behind her on the ground as her legs were extended in front of her. She tilted her head to one side and shut her eyes. When she opened them, her gaze went straight to the old swing that was almost, but not quite, hidden behind the big trunk of the tree. Wide-eyed she exclaimed, "Can I play on dat?!" She excitedly pointed in the direction of the swing with the wooden seat.

Pleased she had spotted it, I nodded approvingly and said, "Yes, of course!" And in an instant, she was in the swing doing the necessary pumping of legs and leaning back in order to build the necessary momentum of a perfect rise and fall. The thing was though that her swing remained relatively motionless despite all her efforts. She was trying hard to almost will the swing into motion, but to no avail.

"Here, let me push you to get you started?" I asked as I hopped up to give her a push. One gentle push, then two, then three, and then Tabitha was in flight and in control of her own easy to and fro. "Now you're flying! Great job!" Encouraging her was my gift to her. I fully intended to do much more of that.

"Tabitha," I began. "Do you remember the question you asked me yesterday?" My heart was racing just a bit with the desire to give her an honest answer in a way she could understand.

"Uhhhh, hmmm ...," she muttered as she still enjoyed the light wind against her skin. Her long ponytail was blowing behind her, and then into her face, as she continued to pump her little legs in a smooth rhythm.

"You asked me about your "other" mommy and why she decided to not keep you." The words stuck in my throat saying them out loud. As I gazed upon this sweet, beautiful girl, I only wanted to empower and nurture her growing spirit.

"Do you know who I am, Tabitha?" I waited for her answer in an anxious moment until she responded.

"Yes!" she cried in an affirmative tone. "You're the nice lady who swings me real good!" She giggled as if she were enjoying an ironic joke she'd just told.

I began slowly, "Tabitha, have you ever felt both happy and sad at the same time?" I was trying in earnest to be relatable to a five year old.

"That sounds funny! How can I be *bof* at the same time?!" Tabitha said as she scrunched up her nose.

"Yeah, I know, the thought kinda doesn't make any sense, right?" I kept going, in-between continuing to give her a couple of pushes on the swing when she'd lose speed. Pausing to push her also gave me time to carefully hand pick my words so she might find meaning and understanding in them. The concept of holding both joy and sorrow at once is a difficult one to find the words to express. Many adults can't comprehend the feeling either — either it's all good, or all bad.

For me, when I tried to stop thinking that way, it was as though an alternate universe opened to me to be able to see shades of gray. While not always easy, and so often it's not, I've begun to see how *every thing* belongs. And I was about to attempt to explain this esoteric reality to a five year old.

"Do you ever think about when Tabby was a kitten? Do you remember what she looked like? Or what size she was?" As I spoke these words, we both turned to admire Tabby who was still on the blanket enjoying the warm sunshine while she watched her beloved owner swinging on the old rope swing.

"She was soooo little and fluffy! She used to fit in my mom's hat box lots better than now. Daddy says she's a fat cat!" Tabitha said these last words in a way which clearly indicated she disagreed with her father's assessment. Then she brightened again saying, "She's *my* kitty, and I love her!"

Leading up to explain to her an example of what bitter-sweet means, I said, "Do you ever miss her being a kitten?"

"Yeah, kittens are sooo cute," Tabitha giggled.

"So, are you saying that you wouldn't trade the all-grown-up cat that Tabby is now in order to get another kitten?" I was trying to lead her to an understanding of sorts.

"No, I'd never give my Tabby cat away. Not even for a cute kitten." She continued, "Nope, nope, I wouldn't!" She looked as though this thought was affecting her on a visceral level. She folded her arms tightly around herself as if for comfort.

"Are you sad you'll never see her as a kitten again, except in photographs?" "Well, yeah," she hesitated before going on. "I'm a little sad, but happy she's all growed up. We can do lots more together now," Tabitha locked eyes again with her pet and looked as though she might cry.

I let the swing come to a complete lazy stop and softly asked, "Would you say you're both happy and a little sad that Tabby is no longer a kitten?" I waited for a sign of recognition to show on her face.

She tilted her head to one side, looked at me with her clear blue eyes, and slowly nodded her head up and down. "Yep, I'm bof happy and sad."

"And you know what, Tabitha? I think it's OK to feel both of those feelings at the same time. I'm so proud of you for being here with me. I like talking with you," I said as I gave her soft hair a light stroke down her long light brown ponytail.

"It makes my heart feel like it's beeping. It beeps when I feel sad. And it beeps sometimes when I'm happy, too," Tabitha said looking down at her small, sneakered feet as she continued to sit on the slightly swaying swing.

"I understand," I said softly. "When you think about your first mommy – how does *that* make you feel?"

"Sad," Tabitha said. "I feel real sad sometimes."

"Losing things we love *is* sad," I said. "I'll bet losing you made your "other" mommy real sad, too. But her deciding to not be your mommy had everything to do with her, and very little to do with you."

"Huh?" Tabitha looked at me with eyebrows raised and in question.

"She somehow came to the idea that *she* was not worthy of *you*. It wasn't a question of whether she loved you enough, or too little. It was more that she didn't trust herself to be able to take care of you. She didn't know her own worth. That's why she gave you to your parents. She was convinced that they must certainly be better able to take care of you than she would be."

"But she didn't even know my mommy and daddy! How could she think that?"

I didn't answer. That would be a conversation for another day.

Tabitha continued, "Please don't tell my mommy and daddy though about me missing "other" mommy. They'd be *real* mad. I would get in twouble." She looked anxiously around her surroundings at The Gathering Place to see if anyone was listening as if her parents may be close by and judging her harshly.

"Tabitha, you're safe with me. I won't let any harm come to you. You aren't in danger," I said each of these words very slowly and distinctly. And then, I repeated them for a second time, "You are in no danger." I tried convincing her to feel free and unrestricted. Still, I could tell she was fearful and afraid her honesty may backfire. She was acting as if the green and gold grassy hills and trees had ears in which to hear.

"My mommy hits me when I ask about my "other" mommy. She says I'm lucky and special to have been picked by 'em," Tabitha said in a low whispery voice. "I'm afraid of mommy."

I looked sweet Tabitha in her eyes, then leaned down to put my hand soothingly on her back and said, "I see you, little one. I hear you. What you're saying matters so much to me. Keep going."

"I wish you were my mommy!" she said as big fat tears sprang from her eyes and rolled down her flushed pink cheeks.

Now I was holding her tight. I felt each shudder of Tabitha's little body as she let her emotions flow. In my mind and in my heart, I was saying, "I am, little one. *I'm* your mommy now. Welcome home."

# CHANGING THE TRAJECTORY OF MY LIFE

*My journey has always been the balance between chaos and order.*

— PHILIPPE PETIT
HIGH-WIRE WALKER BETWEEN THE TWIN TOWERS

In my profession as a personal trainer in fitness, there's an important term called "proprioception." Simply put, it's the sense of self-movement and body position. It's sometimes described as the "sixth sense." When talking with clients, I always like to use the example of: if you were walking on a flat concrete sidewalk, and then had to suddenly step off into the soft grass, proprioception is your body's innate ability to adjust to the new surface. Most of us would be able to adjust to the new information of suddenly walking on a new surface, however, someone who has poor proprioception may trip or fall. As an adoptee, it's as though my psychological proprioception, or my ability to know where I am in space and time, was altered. So much effort has been put into trying to orient myself within my world. Instead of being able to move freely without the hypervigilance of consciously and consistently thinking about my environment, I have often felt as though I have been in a freefall ever since my birth.

My life and being an adoptee are inextricably linked. It's the lens for which I view everything. I guess that's fair to say since I have no reference as to what not being relinquished feels like. I have struggled long and hard to not let it define me, for I am so much more than being the eternally adopted child. Infantilism is a common mindset of both adoptees and society categorizing them as children. But those adoptees grow up — even though the stigma of having been a child remains. Once adopted, always adopted. The phenomenon of adoption moves through all the many life developmental stages of the adoptee until they pass. Even then, there's the generational effects of adoption that transfer to their children, and to their children, and beyond.

Instead of letting it conquer me, I like to think I've converted my adoption angst into being the fire in my belly. That same fire has always fostered in me a spirit of resilience and tenacity. I feel as if I was born without a center of gravity, as if my birth mom tossed me in the air with the hope and understanding that my adoptive mom would catch me. Maybe because I had to fight harder to balance my own self made me stronger and more resilient.

In the winter of 1987, I began dating Andrew, who happened to live in the city where my adoption took place. He'd often fly me to visit him. It was casual and not very serious, but he took an interest in my search. He'd offer to help sometimes by looking something up at the library, or getting me an address, or phone number. During one of my visits to see him we started talking in earnest about the letter that my first mom had written to the adoption agency and had signed with her real name.

"What if we were to pay a visit to the adoption agency, you know, after hours? It probably wouldn't be that hard to get in," I said to Andrew. I didn't truly think I would ever be able to follow through with a clandestine plan like that.

"You know, you're probably right. That day you showed me the agency, I could tell the front door was really thin and it didn't look to have any kind of difficult locks. I'm sure a flathead screwdriver would do the trick," Andrew said without hesitation or even blinking. Andrew was a college graduate and business professional at a large beverage corporation. I wouldn't have ever thought him the type to readily entertain getting involved in such risky business.

Rather than saying all the reasons this could be a very bad idea, I found myself saying, "Let's do it."

It truly was as simple as using a flathead screwdriver to pop the locked front door of the adoption agency open. We went in the cover of night with flashlights and even wore the proverbial black clothes, hat, and gloves, too. This was the 1980's, a time before security systems, cameras, and parking lot security guards. It was all very surreal and terrifying. The gravity of the risk I was taking was in the forefront of my mind and had my heart beating thunderously against my chest. It wasn't difficult to imagine the very real possibility of police showing up and arresting me for stealing my own adoption file. My own unamended birth certificate.

The irony hit me as I thought about how adoptees are among the original victims of identity theft due to having their true identity erased, falsified, and expunged. And this practice is legal and accepted by those who had and have a self-interest to do so. As of this writing, only nine states allow adoptees over 18 or 21 unrestricted access to their sealed birth records. In 1987, the time period of my break-in, there were none. While stealing and breaking into anywhere is normally far outside my principles, in this case, I felt very justified.

Once inside the front door, I said, "OK, *now* where?

Where should we start looking?" I hadn't thought this far ahead. While I had been inside this agency when I came to talk to one of the workers, I hadn't had the forethought to check out the layout of the office or determine where 25-year-old adoption records might be kept. And then my sight went straight to a closed door right in front of us. I walked to it and opened the unlocked door to a small closet that turned out to contain two file cabinets and file boxes with lids on the floor.

"You don't think this could be the old files, do you?!" I really couldn't allow myself to think it was going to be this easy. I opened the unlocked top drawer to one of the five-foot-tall file cabinets and was electrified to be looking at adoption records filed by last names listed as A through H, and then by the year of the adoption. In the next moment, however, I clearly saw by the dates listed that these adoption files in the cabinet were much more present day.

While Andrew held the flashlight steady, I turned my attention to the boxes laying on the floor and to the side of the tall file cabinet. They appeared to have writing on them and looked to be labeled in a similar way as the ones in the cabinet.

"*No way!*" I exclaimed. I plunged my gloved hand into a box labeled 1960-1965 and plucked out random boxes that appeared to contain films that were each labeled with adoption years and marked with either A-H, I-P, or Q-Z. I had a moment of doubt thinking "what if I'm at the wrong agency?" But I knew logically that wasn't right because I had talked to the woman from this very agency who had even counseled my birth mother. In the next moment my hope was restored. I found the microfiche film relating to the year of my brother's adoption. 1962. And then I found the film box labeled as adoptions from my adoption year. 1964. Presumably, both my brother's and my personal adoption records should be contained within these files.

"Let me see. Oh my gosh, you found it!" Andrew was almost as excited as I was. But no one could have felt more victorious than me. I felt as though, against all odds, I may have just discovered the holy grail!

All information was stored on microfiche, rather than on a computer system — that technology came much later. Andrew and I made an immediate plan to take the box of films to the closest library. Not wanting to spend one unnecessary second trying to decide which film to take from the box, we made a split decision to take the entire box, hoping it contained both my brother's and my adoption records. And so, with the heavy adoption records in arms, we quickly closed the closet door, and rushed through the agency to exit through the same front door we'd damaged to enter.

Once in the car, Andrew wiped his sweaty brow asking, "What time does the library close?"

We had broken into the agency after they closed at 5:00 p.m. Since it was winter, it had been dark. It was just then after 6:00. "They close at 8:00. So, we really need to hurry," I said feeling frantic and sick with nerves. We had a lot to do in a very short amount of time. I also still felt that the sound of sirens was eminent. I just knew the police were waiting to round us up and take us to jail.

We scanned and scanned through the files after we had settled in at the library's microfiche table. The records were condensed onto multiple rolls of film, which required moving through many, many adoptee names that were not my own. And then it happened. I had finally arrived at my brother's name. Frozen in place, I just stared at his name, his birthdate, and then the name of his adoptive parents. I felt an enormous wave of recognition looking at the adoptive parent's names, since they were none other than my own.

"Andrew," I barely breathed. "This is my brother Tim's adoption file information." My whole body felt on fire at the discovery. The weird thing was even though I knew all of this was unfolding in real time, I couldn't fathom that it actually was.

I started making copies of everything related to his adoption hoping to preserve the vital information in case Tim may want it after I returned home from the weekend. Luckily, Andrew had brought the necessary coins to be inserted into the machine to make each of the copies. I wasn't about to *not* get my brother's file for him when I almost literally had it in my hands. Ironically, when that future time came that I did ask Tim if he wanted his birth information, he replied, "They didn't want me, so why would I want them?"

To find my own name, I had to scroll two and a half years ahead. The same amount as our age difference. It's funny how doubt has a way of creeping in, especially when you feel so close to the finish line. Thoughts of, "What if my adoption didn't get documented?" "What if I didn't grab the right box of adoption records?" "What if..." And then in the middle of these uncertainties, I found what I'd been looking for. It's such a mind-bender of how there are times in your life where you know everything is just about to change. Nothing is ever going to be quite the same again. I almost felt that in that second, the earth actually stood motionless and became so, so, quiet. I had just found my own name with my own birthdate. My knees buckled, barely supporting me to continue standing. I was so incredibly happy, I cried.

The librarian gave us the 15-minute warning of the library closing and we had to shut our research project down. Luckily, I was just finishing up the last of the copies made from the microfiche reader.

"Emma," Andrew warned. "Don't take the time to read

anything now! Just get as much copied as possible. We can read it all later!"

Of course, I knew he was right. I kept plowing forward making copy after copy. The things I was viewing as the screen scrolled by were all the clinical observation notes pertaining to me as an infant, my original birth certificate, and information about my adoptive parents. And then I paused right when Andrew was reprimanding me to hurry and stay on task because I had scrolled to the letter my birth mom had sent to the adoption agency a short time after relinquishing me. It looked just like the typewritten one the adoption worker had provided me with recently — except for one thing. The letter was in her handwriting and, at the bottom of the letter, instead of being a name that had been blacked out, it contained the full handwritten signature of my birth mom.

## SAFETY, TRUST, AND LOVE

*Connectedness has the power to counterbalance adversity.*

— DR. BRUCE PERRY
AMERICAN PSYCHIATRIST, AUTHOR,
SENIOR FELLOW OF THE CHILDTRAUMA ACADEMY

As I continued holding Tabitha in a tight embrace, my mind drifted to a type of alternate reality that I had recently discovered while in a therapeutic counseling session. I've always identified with the idea of allowing a skilled, responsible, and trustworthy counselor to hold that which is too heavy to be carried. I accept and understand their job is to be the guide and the conduit for one to process traumas in a safe environment, where the client's overall wellbeing is of the utmost importance. One of my own issues is that I've always had this feeling of needing to be more than everyone — just to be equal. I'm sure, for me, that this must be just another way in which adoption has colored my life. While this can be a common feeling for a lot of people, it takes on an even deeper level of meaning for an adoptee whose first trauma resulted from the deprivation of being separated from their biology. It's believed there's no time more vulnerable in our lives than in infancy.

For some adoptees, the very first trauma could have possibly been in-utero since the baby was more than likely already deemed unwanted and selected to be relinquished. This trauma is stored and remembered as an unresolved and unprocessed traumatic memory in the brain. In the book *The Body Keeps the Score,* Dr. Bessel van der Kolk states that "trauma is specifically an event that overwhelms the central nervous system, altering the way we process and recall memories."

Eye Movement Desensitization and Reprocessing (EMDR) is a form of psychotherapy that enables people to heal from the symptoms and emotional distress that are still more than likely affecting their adult lives in detrimental ways. It's designed to engage and stimulate both sides of the brain in order to access memories, long-held beliefs and behaviors in order to reprocess them in a new healthier way. Kolk states that EMDR helps integrate traumatic material and "produces a dramatic relief from distress." I became a proponent of this methodology and have seen the deeply healing aspects of it in my own life.

The alternate reality I was meditating on, which my brain created during an EMDR session, was a place of healing. It was the place where The Gathering Place existed. The place where I knew what Tabitha was feeling without even asking her. I knew because I was her, and in some ways, I still *am* her. The difference now though is that I've come to Tabitha with the intent of trying to help her in a multitude of ways. Just as I had so yearned for in my own youth — someone who could help show me the way. I could also possibly help her get a head start on that close-to-impossible Rubik's Cube. I've asked her and the others to come to The Gathering Place so I can be the advocate I never had. Someone who encourages and gives them unconditional love. The kind of love they feel not only in their hearts but in their bones. So, when it comes time to love others, they'll be able to because they know how to love themselves, too.

"Tabitha, what do you say we take a walk? There's a very pretty stream just over the hill and down by a patch of trees. Does that sound fun?" I felt as though I needed to give her permission to leave her present surroundings to distract her from her sadness of thinking about how her mom treats her. In time, we could swing back around and process more. But for now, we *both* could use nature's beauty to soothe our souls and clear our minds.

She gave me a little nod and wiped tears off her cheeks with the bottom section of her white eyelet dress. "Come on Tabby, let's go for a walk," Tabitha said as she scooped her whiskered friend up in an embrace and followed close beside me. It felt so warm with her presence there. I sensed how much she was already trusting me. This was an honor that I absolutely did not want to take lightly.

"I can be a big girl, you know," Tabitha exclaimed. "I don't cry *ALL* the time."

We were winding down the hill to the stream that meandered in a lazy S curve surrounded by lush green grasses. The chilly water was so clear, we could see the array of river rocks lining the bottom of the stream bed. The smooth rocks were glowing with all shapes, sizes, and colors. Just as beautiful were the larger boulders surrounding the stream's edge that were spotted with moss and lichen showing up in vibrant lime green, gray, rust, and yellow. It was enchanting and refreshing.

Taking a deep low belly breath in, I said to Tabitha, "You know, Tabitha, you really *are* OK. What I mean is, there is absolutely *nothing wrong* with you. And there's nothing wrong with you when you cry when you're sad, or when you're scared and want to go to your brother's room for comfort, or when you daydream about your 'other' mommy, or especially when you tell someone how you feel and they in turn intentionally make you feel bad." I continued, "I am so sorry that you've been made to feel that way. It was unfair, unjust, and unloving. The reason I'm here is to help you understand this."

She looked at me bravely and said, "I love you." When she said this, she hugged her Tabby cat even closer.

I leaned my head back letting out a joyous laugh. And then said, "Oh, and I love *you* very much, too!"

"Are you going to leave me? 'Other' mommy left me. And, and, and," she stammered. "My brother, Tim, he doesn't want to play anymore. He says he has other friends now. He wants me to go away cuz I'm a little girl." Tabitha's pain was real. These issues were bigger than what she was able to cope with or understand. She had no one to express these emotions to in order to keep from internalizing every *thing* as her fault.

We paused on the grassy edge of the stream as I began to tell her, "You're *safe* with me, little one! I've asked you to join me so I can share with you my promise that I'm never going to leave you ever again. I know it seems to both you and me that I *have* left you in the past, but I've had an awakening. Please, please forgive me for that. I'm here now. I've come to help you and to be your friend."

How many times I've heard this very promise made to me throughout my life. Promises by the caregivers of my youth to take care of me. It wasn't always physical abandonment. Often it was from emotional abandonment and/or deprivation. I endured this pain from people who were my family, my friends, and from the teachers and principals where I attended school. Attending school after a night of sitting at the family dark hardwood table where I received hours of being dehumanized by my parents, made it difficult to hold it all together at school and appear normal. I so often felt shot full of holes, feeling as though escape was hopeless. Sometimes I would consider and act upon asking for help. I talked to both teachers and principals more than once describing my pain in hopes of causing an intervention. Instead, I was told that if I had more good days than bad, I was doing fine. In addition, by the time I was old enough to go to school, talking with my brother was no longer an option. We no longer trusted each other. My parents had made sure of that by using a divide and conquer fear-based strategy to prevent us from ever forming any kind of positive alliance. I felt truly alone.

"I know these are just words, Tabitha. I mean to *show* you how important you are to me! Will you allow me to do that for you? For us?!" I said as I anticipated her response.

"I want you to stay, nice lady," Tabitha said with a little shy smile. I sensed that her reply was apologetic, saying it in a way that revealed she didn't quite feel she deserved this kindness. I thought, "Oh, little one, what have they done to you? Don't you realize what a sweet, amazing child you are?"

Instead, I said, "Then it's settled!" I cheerfully exclaimed. "The two of us are officially friends!

# SO MANY DISCOVERIES

Difficult roads lead to beautiful destinations.

— GABOR MATÉ
HUNGARIAN-CANADIAN PHYSICIAN, AUTHOR,
LECTURER, CHILDHOOD DEVELOPMENT AND TRAUMA

Andrew and I returned to the car with all the photocopies and the heavy stolen box of films. I was amazed to walk out into the library parking lot and not see the angry flashing lights and loud wailing sirens of police cars. Certainly, we hadn't gotten away with the break in, had we? I threw myself into the car and collapsed. In the dark chilly night, I was using this time to decompress and process the events of the evening. And then it hit me. I stared at the box. And then I stared at Andrew. Suddenly, I had the realization that if I were to keep this box and not return it, many adoptees would never be able to get their own information.

"Andrew?" I said as I was processing these thoughts, "Andrew, we have to return this box. I can't *not* return it. I might as well be stealing from other adoptees just to get my own answers. I can't do that. We have to go back!"

"Well, if we're going to do that, the time would be *now* before tomorrow when they realize there was a break-in. That screwdriver did leave a pretty good mark on the door. I'm sure they'll notice it — especially since we couldn't relock the door when we left," Andrew said. He also seemed resigned to the fact that we needed to go back right then to the scene of the crime. Neither one of us were going to feel OK with keeping other adoptee's files.

As we slowly approached the adoption agency for the second time that night, I again was looking around for police or any signs of unusual activity. I saw nothing. It looked just as peaceful as it had a few hours earlier. There were no lights shining except from the overhead parking lot lights. When Andrew and I were both convinced that it all looked safe, we grabbed the box, our flashlights and the screwdriver. Then after putting back on our black hats and gloves, we began our approach to the door.

"OK," Andrew said in a low voice. "Here we go again." The door resisted only slightly as it made a low groan and then popped open even easier the second time.

There was no guesswork. We knew right where to replace the file box. We were swift and precise in our return of the stolen adoption records. Nevertheless, my central nervous system was in flight mode. I was lightheaded. My palms were sweating, and my heartbeat was pounding in my ears so loudly I could barely hear Andrew say, "And that's it. We've done it! *Let's get outta here NOW!*"

For many days and even years after the event, I feared that I'd get a knock on my door telling me that I'd been caught. That day never came. I often wondered whether the agency ever knew for sure that there *was* a break-in. For robbers, we were very neat and tidy! The only mark we made was a little scrape on the front door that someone may have never noticed. Maybe they even thought a worker had been careless and forgot to lock up that night and that's why the front door was unlocked the next day. Once inside, Andrew and I had made sure there was nothing disturbed or askew. I'm truly grateful that the worst never happened. It could never have happened in the same way in this day and age. I had that in my favor having conducted my search in a less technologically advanced security time of the past.

Once back from my crazy but very productive search weekend, I finally had the luxury of time to spend looking over all my "adoption loot." Among the information were the clinical observation notes taken of me after my birth, and until the time I was adopted. There were even notes on my birth mother during her pregnancy while she was at the maternity home. The thing about curiosity is that it can often lead to finding out information that can be difficult to forget you've seen, once you've seen it. It makes me remember a line from Sue Monk Kidd's book, *The Secret Life of Bees.* "You think you want to know something, and then once you do, all you can think about is erasing it from your mind."

This is an entry from the stolen clinical notes from the agency where I was adopted concerning my birth mother's prenatal care:

```
April 2, 1964
   -   Expectant mother (7 months) was
found to have been attempting to self-
abort.
   -   She has been placed under
observation and ordered bed rest. Both
baby and mother's vital signs have
stabilized.
```

I tried imagining the motives of my birth mom feeling as though that was the best way to solve her unwanted pregnancy. The distress she must have been experiencing to put both herself and her baby in such danger must have been great. My heart ached for her in that moment of reading those words. My next thoughts were of wondering what my own in-utero experience must have been in those moments of peril. I have since read many scientific findings about cortisol, the hormone that a pregnant mother produces under times of stress which in turn is transferred to the fetus. Could that have been my first introduction of experiencing the sympathetic nervous system response of fight, flight, freeze, or fawn mode? Is this where I first developed that implicit sense of being unworthy and a burden to all? When I read the rest of the case notes I felt another chill. I was described as an uncrying, unsmiling, observant and sober baby. The notes also indicated that I was not eating well due to having difficulty with formula. These clinical notes made so much sense to me. And the reason was because all these things would be present in a baby who had endured trauma.

Pressing on, I examined the letter by my birth mom that contained her true identity. I had looked at it earlier but put it away since I was indecisive about the accuracy of the last name. The signature itself was difficult to read and the quality of the old microfiche made its readability even blurrier. I was fairly sure I had the first name right. The last name though was anyone's guess. Remembering what I did next impresses me as I reflect upon where my search led me.

"Hi, I'm calling to inquire if you can help me with a signature that I need deciphered?'" I had looked in the phone book for a local handwriting analysis expert, also called a graphologist. Without a clue as to how reputable this company was, I selected one that was listed and made the call.

"Yes, we do. What do you have for us to look over?" The woman answered. I told her of the letter and that I just needed to have the last name of the author analyzed. We made an appointment for later that week. I felt the panic in my stomach when the woman told me of their exorbitant fees. I agreed to accept the charge regardless.

"The good thing is that we have the body of the letter she wrote in her handwriting so we can get a good idea of how she formed her letters." The expert said as we sat at the small table in her office. She started telling me the things they look for in the analysis process.

"We look for unique qualities such as letters and word spacing, letter and word slant, size and proportionality of letters, flourishes, and other individual attributes," she explained. "If you would leave this letter with me, I'd like to spend the time necessary to get you what you're looking for." I enthusiastically agreed and felt hopeful of this expert being successful.

Over the next few days as I awaited the analysis to be completed, I focused on another important piece of paper. This piece of paper had been forbidden to *me* all my life. Forbidden to me; its subject and rightful owner. My unamended birth certificate. It was indeed mine since the name of the infant was Baby Girl Ridgefort (just as I had found on my adoption decree), born on the day I was born, and in the city of my birth. Chills, chills, chills! I read each word of the information on the document as if it were life giving and I was absorbing its energy through just holding it in my hands. As expected, my birth mother used her fictitious name on the birth certificate document just as she had during her stay at the maternity home. This is exactly why I'd needed the letter my first mom had written to the agency since it was the only documentation regarding my adoption that existed containing her true identity. When I read the entry of the father listed, I heard sirens going off in my head, and then an immediate surge of adrenaline in my veins.

There was a name listed on the document for my birth father. My immediate thoughts were, "What are the chances that this is indeed his name and not something made up?" Well, my next task was to find out.

"Andrew! Can you please look something up in your phonebook for me?" Out of breath, I excitedly asked him when I called long-distance. I was hopeful the person listed as my birth father may still reside in the same city where my adoption took place.

"Sure. What's going on?" Andrew said. I began filling him in on my discoveries. We had not gotten the chance to pour over all that we'd copied from the library that night before I had needed to get back home to my own city.

"Can you please copy the phone book White Pages for this name, *James Adam Lehmann?*" Andrew promised he would and then would place it in the mail to me. Argh, this meant more waiting! In the meantime, I wrote letters to the Department of Motor Vehicles requesting public records of driver's registration information for the person with this name. My plan was to be able to match the two pieces of information with name, birthdate, and residence and phone number.

When I received the phone book listings from Andrew, I literally started calling all the James Lehmann's listed. Surprisingly, there were about 30 individuals listed with that name, or a variation. I was not successful. It wasn't until the DMV information came that a discovery was made. I indeed found a match between the two sources of information, and most importantly, I had a corresponding phone number.

# HEALTHY ANGER TELLS US WHEN THINGS ARE WRONG

*What is to give light must endure burning.*

— VIKTOR FRANKL
AUSTRIAN NEUROLOGIST,
PSYCHIATRIST, PHILOSOPHER,
AUTHOR, HOLOCAUST SURVIVOR

Sitting on the swing alone again at The Gathering Place, I was reflecting on how comforting it had been to be with Tabitha. She and Tabby were off in the distance now playing in the little red wagon. I shut my eyes and began thinking about not thinking at all. Breathing deep breaths with slow exhales. When I meditate, I often have a particular image that helps me slip into a contemplative mood and state of awareness. I see myself in a wooden canoe that's slowly floating down the middle of a wide clearwater river. The terrain of both sides of the deep canyon river are wooded tall green mountains. The fluffy clouds among the blue sky are reflected in the glassy water. As the canoe glides forward, it's as if the bow is silently slicing the body of water in a neat line. This image becomes my stream of consciousness. It's in these silent moments, I feel a connectedness with that which is bigger than myself. A knowingness of purpose and delight that life has a "potential for purpose under any circumstance." These words are by Viktor Frankl, an Austrian neurologist, psychiatrist, philosopher, author, and Holocaust survivor. In his book, *Man's Search for Meaning*, I'm challenged to remember the importance of self-reflection of how my own life has meaning. I've come to realize that it's my choice to do so. The alternative is despair. I often feel that the tension, anxiety, and trauma I've experienced in life has made me search more diligently for clarity and understanding. Through this suffering, I've found meaning.

Deep in thought, and so far away from the old rope swing I presently sat in, I heard a crunching of leaves. I turned my head to see a young girl, maybe around 14 years old. She didn't look me in the eye but stared at the ground. She was dressed in faded jeans, a tee shirt, and her long hair looked lightened by time spent in the summer sun. She stood there with her arms folded tightly across her chest. I was the first to speak.

"Hi there," I began. "My name's Emma. Thanks for coming. I was really hoping you would," I spoke slowly and with respect of knowing just how difficult it was for her to have shown up. This was big. This 14-year-old is one of the most untrusting of all the parts. She didn't answer me. Instead, she started shifting her weight back and forth from one foot, and then to the other. Her gaze also wandered, making sure not to glance at me for too long. It struck me how she seemed a little like a caged animal looking for the closest escape route.

Then she suddenly looked at me and mumbled in a tone of indifference, "I don't know why I'm here." And then she quickly looked away. I viscerally felt her uneasiness. It shot through me flooding me with memories of feeling uncomfortable in my own skin.

I had an idea. Standing slowly, I stepped aside from the swing and made a small gesture for her to take a turn. I looked away as if to give her permission to take the swing at her own pace, or to choose to not sit on it at all. By the time I focused on her again, she was silently sitting in the swing. I witnessed her tension begin to ease as she walked one foot forward on the ground, and then lazily walked the other foot back.

I took a spot on the grassy earth close to her and sat down with my legs bent and crossed. We sat in silence for a good while. I opened my mouth to speak but she beat me to it. "I don't see the point in all this."

"Are you angry..." I paused since I was at a loss of what to call her. "What name shall I call you?"

"Lauren. My name is Lauren," she said with conviction. She continued, "And oh, I'm not *allowed* to be *angry!* That would get me a slap across the face! Or worse!" My gut tightened as Lauren said these words. It took me back to a time in my youth of fear and uncertainty of what would happen next. When you can't trust your caregivers for your safety and/or your basic needs, it definitely changes you as a person. For me, I would try to find other ways to get my needs met. Often putting my faith in people who said that you could trust them, but that ended up not being the case. There'd be many other people in my life who would encourage me to trust them and share my deepest innermost thoughts with, only to realize that I'd been manipulated and even exploited.

I began slowly saying, "Lauren, I'm so sorry you've had to endure this kind of treatment. You...no! *No* child deserves that. Your anger is a normal emotion. Healthy anger tells us when something is wrong." I wanted to tell her that this kind of treatment by her parents was oppressive and very damaging. I also wanted to tell her to know her own worth and to trust herself when something seems off. She seemed to soften a bit at hearing my words. I continued, "What makes you angry? And please remember, I'm not going to judge you for showing your emotions. No matter what they are."

"How can I trust that you won't go tell them everything I tell you?" Lauren shrunk away asking cautiously. "You may say you won't, but then you probably will!" Her face was red and angry tears were forming in her eyes. I could tell she wanted to talk but was convinced that it was too big of a risk to confide in me.

Slowly nodding, I said, "Lauren, I've come to help you and I don't expect you to believe that immediately. I'm willing to take this as slow as you need. You've carried a heavy burden for a very long time and I'm here to show you that you don't have to go this alone anymore." Lauren's brow began to smooth. Her shoulders lowered just ever so slightly, and I even saw her take a deep breath. There, I thought to myself. This was a good beginning.

# HIDDEN IN PLAIN SIGHT

*It is important to expect nothing, to take every experience, including the negative ones, as merely steps on the path, and to proceed.*

— RAM DASS
AMERICAN SPIRITUAL TEACHER,
PSYCHOLOGIST, AND AUTHOR

I traveled back to Colorado Springs again, but this time with my potential birth father's phone number in hand. Andrew picked me up from the airport and we discussed my plan to call James Adam Lehmann as soon as I arrived at my hotel. I only vaguely recall the phone call and what was said. My potential birth father sounded leery about my reason to meet him (I told him I was doing a genealogical search), but he invited Andrew and me to come visit anyway. His small apartment looked only slightly furnished and completely unmatching. It reminded me of a bachelor pad, like maybe he had divorced recently. I wasn't sure. My main goal was to ask him why his name was on my original birth certificate.

James Lehmann was pleasant enough and listened to my

story. I produced my original birth certificate and showed him where his name appeared. "Do you know why your name is on my birth certificate?" I ask him.

"Hmm, no I don't really know." He seemed to be indulging me by looking at the document briefly and then shrugged his shoulders.

I explained to him, "My birth mother listed on this document used a fictitious name. I have recently found out that her real first name is or was Ruth. I'm currently waiting to have an expert confirm her last name. I have it, but I can't make it out." Then I showed him the signature I had of my birth mom's.

"Did you know a person named Ruth here in Colorado Springs in 1964?" I thought I saw a slight shift in his composure.

"Well, yes, maybe— I don't really remember her. I only did it to help out a friend," James said casually and offered no more.

"You put your name on my birth certificate to just help out a friend?" I repeated. I was trying hard to absorb this information. It made no sense to me.

"What was Ruth's last name?" I asked.

"No, I don't remember her or who I helped. I'm sorry," James said with a polite smile, "but I'm not your dad." He said these words looking me square in the eye.

We talked a little longer and he pretended to be interested in my life even though he'd just claimed to be a stranger to me with no connections. I didn't press him any further with questions. I accepted defeat. Looking back, I find it peculiar that he hugged me goodbye. What James Adam Lehmann didn't know on that day that I met him was that in 34 years, there was going to be a source that's 100% accurate in identifying DNA. He didn't know I was going to be able to spit in a tube and pay for a service that could confirm whether he was or wasn't my biological father.

I left James Lehmann's apartment that day having an innate feeling that he was my biological father. There were a few traits and features I was basing this on, but there was one that I felt very telling. I've always had thick black prominent eyebrows. This was the first feature I noticed about James. I also noticed we shared an athletic body type and were similar in height, weight, hair color and complexion. The later features could be a coincidence, but the clincher was the shared black bushy eyebrows.

Back again in my hometown, I tried to process the meeting I'd had in Colorado Springs over the weekend. I was unsure of how to proceed. And then shortly after, I heard from the handwriting analysis expert.

"Emma, I believe I've deciphered the full name on the letter you provided. Can you come today to review our findings?" The graphologist said.

Feeling less than successful after meeting my potential birth father, James, I was ready to receive this good news. "Of course! I'll be over during my lunch hour? Around noon?" That was two hours from then. Considering how electrified my body felt at hearing this, I was unsure how I could maintain until then.

Sitting at the same small table we had before, she produced the letter and set it before us. My skin felt as though it was pulsating with every heartbeat. I wanted to grab the letter, skip to the end, and finally see what my birth mother's name was. But instead, the graphologist began telling me specific things about the letters she viewed and used terms I was unfamiliar with. My heart was racing so fast it made it difficult to follow her. As it seemed she was winding down in her explanation of letter structure, I heard her finally get to the first name of the author. She confirmed I had the first name correct. It was *Ruth*.

"Starting with the first letter of the last name, I was able to find a consistency with the same letter that showed up in the text section. I determined that the letter is *J*. Do you see how the capital letter *J* is written with a big lower loop? This indicates creativity, imagination, and a person who has a lot of friends."

Until then, I'd never realized how much a person's handwriting supposedly says about their personality. Based on this, was I to consider that my birth mom would be a friendly, creative sort? A loyal friend to others, but yet a stranger to her biological daughter?

"The author writes in what we call the 'middle zone' which means they are probably social, and their day is taken up by their relationships. This dominant middle zone writing style is common among people in their 20's who don't have any long-term plans and all their energy goes into their social life. These writers usually have very developed social skills. The author's letters are also moderately closely spaced together which indicates that they can handle people being close to them, as opposed to someone who writes their letters small and widely spaced apart."

I had another pause in reflecting how painful this was to hear. I was trying to understand possibly having a birth mother who is potentially close with most people, but just not with me. Paradoxically speaking, this was fitting right along with the frustrations of trying to advance on my Rubik's Cube mystery. I suddenly felt as though I were a contestant on *The Wheel of Fortune* television game show with Vanna White slowly turning around each tile revealing the next letter. And me, chomping at the bit to solve the puzzle.

"Do you see the shape of this next letter, which is *o*? There are two in the last name. What I'm looking at is the fullness of the letter that indicates this person is most likely extroverted in nature, talkative, and open in her dealings. Similarly, another letter, which is *a,* is also more open showing the writer has vital strength and hope."

"The letter *h* is shaped in a way that shows a less practical and more creative approach. Usually, this means it takes more time in decision making."

"There are also two *n*'s in the last name. *N* is known to be associated with the intellectual trait of a person. For this writer, the *n* is larger and expresses an outgoing person who has joy for life."

I was thinking, "Cut to the chase already! What is her last name?!" I didn't want to hear how great she was person-to-person, or at least to most.

"And the final lowercase letter to discuss, and there are two again, is the letter *s*. Traditionally, this letter is associated with 'moral consciousness'. The shape and curve of this writer's *s* indicates a fighting spirit, combative consciousness, and is generous," she said.

"In conclusion, the last name in question is *Johansson.*" The graphologist said this last statement and then put her pen down. "I am 99.9% sure."

# THE HEALING RHYTHM OF WATER

*No one belongs here more than you.*

— BRENÉ BROWN
AMERICAN RESEARCHER,
STORYTELLER, PROFESSOR, LECTURER,
AUTHOR, AND PODCAST HOST

I took Lauren on the same walk down by the river that I had with Tabitha. Nature seems to be a universal language that all can agree on its wonder and beauty. Once down by the bank, we could hear the steady meditative flow of the water and feel the cool breeze. Spotting a small mint colored frog with metallic-like green stripes perched on a rock, I walked a little closer and pointed so Lauren might see it. She surprised me by allowing herself to clearly be enchanted. We watched the frog sunning himself and then suddenly hop into the stream making just the tiniest splash. I wondered how the frog innately knew where he was going. What he'd do next. I guessed it had to be mostly instinct leading the frog forward to his next steps without involving reason.

"So, where've you been? I've been really kinda needing you around," Lauren asked in an accusatory way. "It's like I've been left to figure all this shit out on my own. It sucks. Why did my parents even adopt children if they didn't want to be bothered by them?" It was a fair question.

"I know this probably doesn't help, but I've been here all along. I needed to figure a lot out first to come back and be of any help to you. I'll bet that sounds confusing." I took some deep breaths before going on. "I had to learn some hard lessons of how to choose me, *us*, first. Once I figured out that life wanted me, *I* had to learn to want *me*. I promise you, I tried to get back to you as soon as I could. I'm sorry it probably wasn't fast enough," I said. I felt my tears spill down my cheeks.

"It's just," Lauren paused. "It's just that I'm so alone and sad. I'm sad most of the time." It was hard for her to complete the sentence. Tears were welling in her own eyes.

"Thanks for being able to share that with me, Lauren. Do you know that's the first step to taking care of yourself? Showing your own self love and care? I'm going to be here now, whenever you want me, and I'm going to be listening. I'm hoping you'll keep sharing all your thoughts and feelings with me because I'm here to tell you *that you matter.*"

I wanted so much to hug and assure her that I meant what I was saying. In the past, I'd abandoned myself so many times all due to fear of disappointing others. Placing others needs before my own and thinking I was undeserving to receive the same grace that others get freely. I'm not alone in this type of adoptee syndrome of internalizing guilt and shame. The prevailing narrative of adoption is that adoptees should feel grateful that someone wanted them to raise "as if they were their own." This statement alone insinuates that we are not *real* but more a substitute for the real thing. As a result, many adoptees struggle with identity issues and feelings of low self-worth. When the first relationship we've ever known abandons us (for whatever reasons), it's experienced as being unwanted and unloved.

"No one's ever said something like that to me before," Lauren said with her eyebrows raised a bit. "I've never thought I was that bad a kid, but my parents always say I'm ungrateful and selfish."

"I'm going to tell you something. You may not factually know this now, but you do know within yourself that your parents are dealing with their own inadequacies. Their behavior has nothing to do with you or your brother. They're what's called emotionally immature and have chosen to not do the hard work it takes to develop themselves or resolve their own traumas. The result is that they take out their fears, frustrations, failures, and their own issues of feeling lesser than, on you."

I went on to say, "It's not right. It's not fair. But this is who they are. Your challenge is to stay strong and know that who you are is good. Adoption means that others made decisions about your life that you had no control over, and it means that you came into this world without the glue of connectedness that others usually get in order to thrive. It's as though you were pulled by the root and severed from everything and everyone you'd ever known. This was not your fault! Don't let them de-self you into thinking *you* can ever be anyone other than *you*. I can say it won't be easy, especially when they'll be sending the message that you're not good enough as you are. This is when I want you to *know* your worth."

"I don't know how to survive. My mom screams, and hits, and slaps me all the time. She and my dad sit us at the kitchen table almost every night and tear us to shreds. Usually after they've been drinking, but not always. It's so hard to go to school the next day, trying to act normal, after I've cried all night," Lauren confessed.

I moved closer and just stood with her. We stared at the moving water of the stream as it flowed continuously forward in a rhythm all its own.

"It hurts. I know." It's all I could say to validate Lauren. "In those times and beyond, I'd like you to hold your truth close. The truth is that who you are is good.

The truth of how resilient you are. The truth that even though you may feel despair, your spirit is strong and will endure."

Lauren was crying now with her head hanging low. I put my arms around her and felt her pain, for I had been there. And had lived through it.

I was 17 years old before having the guts to rear back my own arm ready to strike after my mother had landed consecutive powerful blows to my cheek and left her deep fingernail marks. Dazed and cringing from the hot stinging of my left cheek, I glared at my mom and huffed out a huge cry. By the time I had righted myself, she came in with another *slap!* And then followed by another *slap, slap!* The last slap hit the back of my head since I'd long since learned how to pivot and duck her swings. It was at that moment that something snapped within me. I barely recognized my own voice when an angry guttural sound came rumbling up from deep within me. I'd finally found my voice to say with conviction, "DON'T YOU *EVER, EVER* HIT ME AGAIN!" It was as if all the years of her hitting me and then me having to stuff all the hurt and pain down within me, came out like an erupting fountain of fire. It was a voice that I'd finally found and had suppressed for far too long. My mother never hit me again.

Friedrich Nietzsche, the German philosopher, essayist, and cultural critic, said "He who has a *why* to live can bear almost any *how*." To me this says our suffering has a purpose.

According to Nietzsche, "suffering is the only thing that bestows value upon the world. Without pain and misery, life would be absurd and worthless." I think I understand the contrast that this represents: you need to have experienced suffering to be able to recognize joy. Learning how to choose joy is a revolutionary act and a gift of love. Or, if there were no choices, what would be the purpose? Maybe it's that tension between all things that's necessary to make things whole.

And, maybe some women are just not meant to be mothers because self-serving, egocentric love is really no love at all.

# THE DISCOVERIES CONTINUE

*In wisdom gathered over time I have found that every experience is a form of exploration.*

— ANSEL ADAMS
AMERICAN PHOTOGRAPHER

Ruth Ann Johansson. My birth mother's name. I confirmed her middle name by finding it on public record at the library in the census records. I also had found her place of birth, a little village founded in 1871 in Nebraska called Dannebrog. It's called the Danish capital of Nebraska because it was founded by Lars Hannibal, president of the Danish Land and Homestead Company which was to secure a tract of land for settlers of Danish origin. I decided the best place to start would be to call the Archives and Tourist Center of Dannebrog. I also knew from the non-identifying information I had received from the adoption agency that Ruth had seven other brothers and sisters. A family that size would most likely be known in a town of only 300 residents.

"Hello, thank you for contacting the Village of Dannebrog. How may I help you?" A woman answered.

"Hello, I was hoping you might be able to help me locate a large family that lived in Dannebrog back in the '50's? I'm working on a family tree project and have been told of relatives I have in your village. Is there someone I might be able to talk with?" My heart was doing that all-too-familiar pounding again: this could possibly be how I would find the Johansson family. And that would lead to Ruth.

"Let me have you speak to Carol. She's lived here all her life and might be able to help you. Hang on a minute, honey," the nice woman said.

"Hi, this is Carol. May I help you?" Another woman's voice said a few moments later.

I was hurriedly forming sentences in my head to ask. "Um, yes. Thank you. I'm doing a genealogical search and have been told of relatives that I have there in Dannebrog?"

"What's their name, dear? I've lived here in Dannebrog all my life," Carol confirmed.

My throat constricted and my tongue felt thick, but I managed to say, "The Johansson family? They would have lived there in the 50's?"

"Hmm, Johansson. I know a few by the last name of Johnson." My heart fell to my feet at her words. She continued saying, "Why don't you call the diner on Main Street? They've been in business since the 40's and everyone in Dannebrog has passed through there at one time or another." My hopes had been dashed and then restored in all of 30 seconds. She kindly gave me the phone number of the local diner and I made that my next call.

The phone rang six or seven times before someone picked up. "Dannebrog Diner," a woman's voice sang out. I could hear music, the clatter of dishes, and loud random voices in the background. I pictured a crowded restaurant with formica tables and counter tops matched with red vinyl booths and stools.

"Hi, I don't mean to bother you, but I was told by the Dannebrog Tourist Center that someone that works at the diner might know of some relatives of mine that I'm looking for?" I started to hold my breath unsure what the next few moments might bring.

"Who you lookin' for?" She asked matter-of-factly.

"I'm looking for a family by the name of Johansson in the area?" I said for the second time that night.

"Oh, do you mean June Johansson? She ain't workin' tonight." She paused to tell someone in the diner that their food was "coming right up" and then redirected her attention to me. "What's your number, hon, and I'll have her call ya?"

"That would be great! Thank you so much," I said and hung up after giving her my phone number. I'd been so nervous I hadn't even asked the woman at the diner anything about who this June Johansson was. For all I knew, she wasn't even related to Ruth at all. Now I had to wait for someone named June to call me.

I was feeling so close to my answers now I could almost taste it. My search had started to consume me, and I could think of little else. It was just a matter of time before I would know a good portion of my narrative. Somehow, I knew that to understand it all was going to take a lifetime. I was beginning to understand that, while finding out my birth parents' names would help, it was not going to fix everything. I'd not even come close to realizing yet how much more I'd need to learn before finding a reasonable amount of peace.

I didn't have to wait long before my home phone rang, and I was talking to someone who introduced herself as June Johansson. "Hello?" I said.

"May I please speak with Emma? This is June Johansson

from Dannebrog, Nebraska calling." Her voice was warm and mature.

"Yes, this is her...thanks for calling back! I wasn't sure you'd get the message." I admitted.

"Oh yes, I wanted to get back to you quickly. I understand you're looking for my family?" June said.

"You're a Johansson?" I asked her, almost panting.

"Well, that's my maiden name, dear. My married name is Mortenson," June said, sounding as though she wanted to be helpful.

Her tone sounded safe and inviting to me. I felt compelled to continue to ask her my real question.

"Do you happen to know of a woman by the name of Ruth Ann Johansson?" I let that question just hang out there. I was barely breathing.

"Oh, my goodness, dear. Ruth is my youngest sister."

I felt the earth shift underneath my feet. What did June just say? I answered myself in my head, *she said that Ruth is her youngest sister*. OK, breathe and proceed, I told myself.

"Do you know how I might get a hold of her?" I squeaked out. All I could hear was the sound of my heart pounding wildly, so it was hard to pay attention to June's words.

"Ruth lives in California now. I can give you her number. Do you have a pen, dear?"

## KATE VISITS THE GATHERING PLACE

*The journey to happiness involves finding the courage to go down into ourselves and take responsibility for what's there: all of it.*

— RICHARD ROHR
AMERICAN AUTHOR, SPIRITUAL WRITER,
AND FRANCISCAN FRIAR

The late afternoon sun at The Gathering Place was warmer today. It felt good as I turned my face upward, eyes closed toward the sky. I was taking a little time to reflect on all I'd learned so far from both Tabitha and Lauren. Being their advocate is exactly what I longed to be. I knew how much courage it had taken for them to have accepted my offer to join me, and I was proud of them and knew they were feeling a new sense of hope and purpose to their lives. I was eager to share even more with them. My desire to spend more time with them grew exponentially as we began to trust each other more.

My next guest was on her way up the dirt path that led to the big old oak tree. Her gait was brisk and looked like someone with an agenda. She had light colored khaki pants, a light blue Polo button-down shirt, and dark leather loafers with tassels. She looked every bit like 18-year-old me in my sophomore year of college.

She approached saying, "Hi, I'm Kate. I wanted to come see what you wanted? You called for me?"

"Hi, Kate. So glad to see you," I said with my body fully facing hers for a welcoming greeting.

"Yeah, well, I felt I owed it to you to listen to what you have to say," She wasn't unpleasant, but her energy definitely indicated she wasn't interested in having a long conversation.

I paused a moment before saying, "I just wanted to check in with you and see how you're doing? I hear you're off to college now?"

"That's right. I'm finally out of that house and can make my own decisions now," Kate said as she kept her arms tightly folded across her chest.

"I see. It must be difficult to suddenly have that kind of freedom. You know, to just be yourself now after you've had to change yourself for so many years just to survive in your childhood home." I was talking straight with her, looking her square in the eyes, and not wasting any time.

"Oh, I can do it just fine. I don't need any help if that's why you're here," Kate declared. She acted as though she might turn around and leave any minute. Instead, she started to list the things that were good in her life now, "I have a boyfriend. I live in a different city than my parents. I go to parties. I do whatever I want now – I'm doing great."

"That's wonderful. May I ask you something though?" I chose my words carefully. "Are you ready to start talking about your pain and confusion of what bothers you so deeply?"

"It doesn't affect me anymore. All that childhood stuff — if that's what you're talking about. I've left all that behind.

What good would talking about it now do anyway? Have you forgotten? We've tried that and we've just been made to feel like it's all in our head and it's all our fault. Don't you remember talking to that school principal in fifth grade when we had to move and go to a new school? We were put in an underachiever's class. We told mom, *and* dad, and they acted as though we were exaggerating. Then – and *then,* when we talked to the principal, he just patted us on the head and told us nothing could be changed. We had to stay at that level for two years! What bullshit that was!" Kate was placing her fingertips up to her forehead as if it ached.

"I do remember that. And yes, it was BS. I'd like to suggest you might be able to see things more clearly by talking things over with others and learning how to trust again. This could help you in making the better choices you really want in the future. Choices that aren't made by a wounded part of you that might not be operating in your best interest," I offered gently.

"Thanks, but all I want to do now is have fun. Don't I deserve that?" I thought maybe she was going to clam up, but then she continued, "I do worry all the time though about my boyfriend Mark leaving me. I think I drive him a little crazy with how I make him tell me he loves me all the time."

"Does he give you any reason to think he might leave?" I asked Kate.

"Well, no. It's just this feeling I have in the pit of my stomach that makes me worry he *could* leave me at any time. I get very upset when he wants to go out with his friends. I'm embarrassed to say how I spy on him sometimes. I can see his fraternity house from my bedroom window in my sorority house. I watch him walking to his car leaving the parking lot with his friends for a night out and I just cry." Lauren paused, and then continued, "Sometimes I wait at that window until he comes home."

"Why do you think you do this, Kate?" I gave her the time she needed to reflect on my question.

"I don't know," she said, knitting her eyebrows together. "He tells me all the time how much he loves me, but I still feel heartbroken. One time, we had an argument in his car on the way home from somewhere and we sat in front of my house for at least an hour. He kept telling me he'd see me the next day and that we were OK even though we'd had a disagreement. But for some reason I couldn't force myself to just call it a night and get out of his car. He was exhausted by trying to console me and asking me to please get out of the car so he could go home. I don't even know what that was all about." Kate had a faraway look on her face.

"How would you describe the pain if you could put words to it? Where do you feel it in your body?" I asked.

"I feel it in my gut. It feels like I'm desperately trying to survive – to breathe. It feels all consuming," Kate said as she touched her heart with one hand and her stomach with the other.

I nodded knowingly, "Does it feel like self-preservation to you?"

Kate stared at me. Her eyes were becoming watery. "Yes. Yes, it does. In those times, it feels like it's the most important thing in the world. As if my life depends upon it."

"Kate, have you ever felt this way before?" I moved over to the swing and pointed to it in case she cared to have her turn. I hoped so. I know for myself that when I sit in it, my body immediately feels looser, freer. Kate took a seat on the swing and didn't look as anxious to leave The Gathering Place as she had when she'd first arrived.

"Yes, it's a familiar feeling I've had all my life. A feeling of being unsafe, unloved, and like I don't have a clue of how to rescue myself from free falling.

Kate paused and then said, "Yes, I think it's all connected.

It's like I've been looking for a safe place to land all my life. A safe home."

I smiled and said, "That is so insightful! It also happens to be the truth. Kate, that's why I'm here. I've come to show you and the others, how strong we can be together. How we can all help one another feel safe, feel loved, and no longer be in a freefall. Life wants us. I want us. Do *you* want us?"

Kate had been dragging her feet on the ground as she sat in the swing, but now she was lifting her feet up off the ground. Pretty soon she was pumping her legs and doing an easy swing back and forth. I may have even seen a slight smile cross her face.

# A SOLID ROW OF THE RUBIK'S CUBE COMPLETED

*Most people stop looking when they find the proverbial needle in the haystack. I would continue looking to see if there were other needles.*

— ALBERT EINSTEIN
THEORETICAL PHYSICIST

I did not call Ruth the day her older sister June gave me her number in California. I didn't even call her the next day. I was devising exactly what I'd say to her. I was imagining a thousand different scenarios of what I'd say or what she'd say. Of course, there was also the possibility that I might even have the wrong Ruth. I kept going over the facts again, and again. On the third day, I went home from work for lunch. It was finally time to place the phone call and see what would happen. Sweating and my heart pounding, I picked up the phone and dialed.

"Hello?" A woman's voice answered.

"May I please speak with Ruth?" I squeaked out.

"This is Ruth," Her voice sounded a little muffled and unclear. I pressed forward regardless.

"Hi, my name is Emma. Do you have a moment to talk?" I asked timidly.

"Well, yes. What's this about?" Ruth asked hesitantly.

"I have something important to ask you and I want to make sure that you're ok to speak freely," I stammered. I was more concerned with her feelings than my own. All I kept thinking was how much I was about to disrupt her life.

Again, she said, "What's this about?"

This was the moment. My search had led me into this liminal space of unknowing and knowing, and in between them, was this door. I pressed forward saying, "My name at birth was Baby Girl Ridgefort. I was born in Colorado Springs, Colorado on July 21, 1964. I was relinquished and then adopted by my parents."

Silence. And then I heard Ruth crying. The rest of the conversation was difficult to understand due to her tears inhibiting her to speak clearly. But I *did* have my confirmation. She said she'd always known I'd come looking for her and was happy that I had. This was not a long conversation, but it was long enough for me to feel emotionally drained and as if I'd run a marathon. I then offered to fly to San Juan Capistrano, a little sleepy coastal town in California, just south of Laguna Beach in Orange County, to meet her. I asked if she'd like that, and she said she would. The end of the conversation was me saying I'd let her know as soon as I could put the trip together.

After the phone call to my birth mother, I sat on the floor and tried to absorb it all. My thoughts were a jumble of facts, feelings, and of all the physical effort it had taken to get to the point where I was – right at that moment. Wonder and amazement were swirling around in my mind, body, and soul. I also felt a new sense of confidence in myself that I had indeed found the "needle in a haystack." Truly an almost impossible feat. At that moment sitting on the floor of my single bedroom apartment, I felt I had just accomplished a whole solid row on my Rubik's Cube.

My next step was to call Andrew in Colorado Springs and tell him everything. He was almost as excited as I was. Looking at the calendar, we decided to fly to California in a couple of weeks. I was grateful to have Andrew since he honestly seemed invested in helping me with my search. He'd been there through almost the entire process. And how perfect it had been that he lived in the city where I'd been born and was in the location of where my adoption information was up to that point.

I wore a solid white tea-length sundress to meet my birth mother for the first time. Our place of meeting turned out to be an alcohol rehabilitation center where Ruth was currently residing. At 24 years old, I didn't know much about what that all meant. It was very foreign to me, but I was still so eager to meet her.

When I got to the center, I was led to an amazingly picturesque outdoor area. Off in the distance was a clear view of the beautiful blue Pacific Ocean. We sat on an outdoor bench feeling the ocean breeze and warm sun. After the first hug I've ever received from my birth mom, we started a volley of questions back and forth. During our conversation, I stepped back in my mind noticing that Ruth and I looked nothing alike. It was difficult to know whether the differences were from our biology or from the apparent hard life she had lived. It was clear there had been years of neglect to her personal appearance caused by lack of care. Nevertheless, I was so happy to be sitting with my birth mom, knowing that I'd fought such a valiant fight in order to make the unknown known.

I began to notice that Ruth was not a straight talker. She seemed to talk in riddles and be evasive in her communications, making her hard to understand. I began tiring of the reunion. I was having to work too hard to gather practically any information from her. It was frustrating and I felt no reciprocity in our communication.

"Is James Adam Lehmann my biological father?" I asked after we'd been speaking of my fantastical story of how I found her. She seemed genuinely impressed by the lengths to which I'd gone to discover my adoption story.

"Who's that?" She said with eyebrows raised and her forehead wrinkled.

"He's who's named as my biological father on my original birth certificate," I said in a confused tone. Internally, I felt a surge of panic that Ruth appeared to not know who I was speaking of.

"Oh, no, hmm...I don't know," she mumbled.

"I'm sorry, what does that mean? He's not my father? Do you know him?" I said, searching for clarification. My feelings of frustration were hard to hide.

"That name doesn't sound familiar," Ruth stared blankly.

I was unsure of how to proceed with this conversation. "James Lehmann told me that he authorized his signature on my birth certificate only to help out a friend. Did you know him?"

"I may have. What was his name again?" she replied to me. I let the conversation drift off after I realized she was not going to answer any of my questions.

And then she said, "I have a son named Steve. He's 18 years old. He takes care of me because he knows how much I need him."

"So, he's my half-brother?" I asked.

"His father and I married. Or at least I think he was the father. That's how my last name changed from Johansson to Curtis." Ruth said.

"But we don't share the same father, do we?" I was totally

confused and exhausted from expending so much energy trying to communicate with Ruth.

"No, at least I don't think so..." she said as her voice trailed off.

I began regretting this reunion and started remembering things that some friends had said prior to me coming to California to meet my birth mother for the first time. "Be careful what you wish for," and "Don't get your hopes up too high," were some of the warnings. But I decided to be happy for the reunion that I was having and to accept it for whatever it was. While I was disappointed that Ruth was not at all who I'd dreamed of her being all my life — she certainly wasn't Samantha from *Bewitched* — I was happy to have found this piece of the puzzle. I found it curious that I kept saying things that made it sound as though I was taking care of her rather than me needing to be comforted by her. It seemed important to me to let her know that I was OK and that she shouldn't worry about me. I was even feeling guilty that I might be living life in a better way than she appeared to be. The woman I'd lived my whole life to meet seemed beyond foreign to me now. The rest of the reunion was surface talk between two strangers.

# PERFECTLY IMPERFECT MIA

*Seek to be Whole, not Perfect.*

— OPRAH WINFREY
AMERICAN TALK SHOW HOST,
TELEVISION PRODUCER, ACTRESS,
AND PHILANTHROPIST

A nine-year-old came to me silently at The Gathering Place. She said her name was Mia. Mia seemed painfully shy and not at all sure of herself. As she looked at the ground, she spoke her first words to me.

"Hi, I'm sorry I'm late." She said this barely above a whisper.

"Mia, you aren't late – you're right on time!" I was hoping to set her at ease.

"I'm sure you have lots of other things to do and if you need me to leave and come back at a better time, I can do that," Mia said, still looking at the ground. Her brows were furrowed and looked as though she were about to cry.

Just then, a gust of wind knocked over my paper cup that I'd set on the surface of a long, flat rock. The water spilled out, covering the rock with wetness that made the light stone change into a deeper shade of mineral-rich gray.

"I'm so sorry!" Mia immediately responded. She was standing closest to the rock where I'd put my water cup, but she was in no way responsible for the wind knocking it over.

"There's nothing to worry about, Mia. Thank you so much for coming," I said reassuringly. "All of the others liked sitting in the swing while they were here. I believe it's your turn!"

Mia followed my instruction as if she felt that's what she was supposed to do. She still avoided eye contact. It made me drift to memories of myself being afraid of looking people in the eyes due to fear that they might actually see me. And if they could look into my eyes, they'd surely see all the ways I'd felt I was flawed. It seemed easier to apologize for taking up too much space and being a burden before others had the chance to discount or dismiss me. One of my worst fears is to be discovered an imposter and told "you don't belong here – you must leave!"

"Thanks for inviting me. I'm sure you have better things to do," Mia said. "At this moment, you are my honored guest, and I don't want to be with anyone or be anywhere other than right here with *you*." I thought I might have seen a shift in composure with Mia's shoulders slightly dropping and allowing her gaze to wander beyond only staring at the ground.

"What do you like to do for fun, Mia?" I asked. She didn't answer immediately, and I gave her all the space she needed to contemplate my question.

"I don't know. Stuff, I guess." She was clamming up. I tried thinking of another way to draw her out and get her to be present with me.

"Are you liking school? Tell me about your friends," I asked.

"I like school alright. It's OK. I like making good grades and getting good report cards. I made all A's last time."

Mia paused and seemed a little exhausted after having spoken that many words to me. Her eyes widened and then she recomposed herself by wrapping her arms around her ribcage as if in retreat.

"My mom and dad say that my brother is really smart. I wish I was as smart as him. I've got a plan though to try even harder next time to get even better grades." Her face changed to having a motivated look of determination written all over it.

"Mia, what do you think would happen if you didn't get all A's?"

She hesitated and said, "The funny thing is ... I don't think much would happen at all. It's like my parents don't expect much from me. They think my brother is the smart one. They just want me to mind them and not ask for too much. So, I don't," Mia said, sounding resigned to perform her dutiful daughter role.

"Do you know what personal boundaries are, Mia?" I asked.

"Um, no, ... I mean, I'm not sure what you mean exactly?" she said seemingly trying to understand and not appear as though she'd just missed an easy question on a quiz.

I treaded lightly, "I know you often feel the need to keep the peace in your family and try to be as pleasing as necessary, but I want to suggest to you that you are deserving of more. Things like being able to say your likes and dislikes without being made to feel bad about it or getting laughed at."

I had her attention, but she seemed as though she wanted to tell me why that wouldn't work for her in the "family dance."

I was well aware of the strict and impossible rules my

parents placed on me during my youth, and how becoming a people-pleaser and a perfectionist were adaptations that allowed me to survive. As an adult, however, these traits have not served me well.

"I'm just not allowed to do that. I would be in so much trouble. Being in that kind of trouble with my parents makes me feel really bad. It's just not worth it." Mia said this as she looked me in the eyes. I was able for the first time to see the depth of her blue-green eyes. I also couldn't help noticing her contrasting thick coal-black eyebrows.

"I know we can't change the past. What happened happened. But I'd like you to know that *future you* gets to decide things for herself. I want you to know that you make it and you do eventually find your voice," I said.

I felt in my bones how much I wanted to give Mia hope. Just as I had needed that hope so badly ever since my trauma of relinquishment at birth. Searching for hope everywhere — and it seemed most often in vain.

Sitting in silence, Mia and I both turned our gaze to a flock of birds flying in their formation in the cloudy blue sky. It struck me in a curious way how it appeared that each bird innately knew how to position themselves. I once learned that the lead flyer in the formation is always changing to conserve energy. The front position is the most taxing, while all the others get the benefit of tail winds of the bird in front of them. When the bird in front gets tired—another takes the lead. The law of physics at play determines the bird's formation.

"Do you ever wish you could fly?" Mia said, watching the birds high overhead.

"I do actually. I often do in my dreams. How about you?" I asked.

"Yeah, me too," Mia said with a little smile. "It's like I can finally breathe when I'm flying in my dreams. It feels great!"

"I've always attributed my fascination of flying with how freeing it would feel to be up so high and see things from that perspective. It feels powerful. And yes, it feels as though I can breathe," I said. "That's what I want for you, you know? I want to help you out of your cage and show you how to fly."

"I would really like that. I would really like that *a lot*," Mia agreed.

# EVERYWHERE I WENT, THERE I WAS

*We're all just walking each other home.*

— RAM DASS
AMERICAN SPIRITUAL TEACHER,
PSYCHOLOGIST, AND AUTHOR

Music served as a life preserver for me as early as kindergarten — it was one of the only ways I could express myself. I gravitated toward a pleasing melody, lots of harmony, and always music that would make me feel something. Music helped me learn how to differentiate my feelings, helping make more sense of my young life. I loved to sing — I loved the feeling of breath in my lungs all the way into my diaphragm and then controlling it with the notes I would sing out into the air. It gave me an understanding of the dual tension it took to hold onto a note at the same time as letting it go. Music has always given me a source of safety and understanding. When I was only 12 years old, and in fifth grade, I was asked to join the high school choir as well as a special singing/dancing performance group. I was beyond happy about this invitation and am thankful — that I had music to help ground me — when there was so much chaos in my life. Music was something that I could pour myself into and find meaning. I was trying to sing myself sane and dance myself free.

Other things that brought me joy and helped me feel safe in my youth were journaling, springboard diving, riding my bike, and going to the pool. Splashing, laughing, the spring of the diving board — these sounds continue to bring me joy.

I looked for meaning and sharing reciprocity in relationships. Reciprocity is like hearing a perfect harmony that fills you up inside. I'd look with great intention to find people who were unique and interesting. I imagine I was also looking for validation from those whom I selected because I had deemed them people to learn from, people who could influence and enhance my life and more than likely, reparent me. There were times I chose well, and there were many times I did not. Almost always, these charismatic people were authority figures — babysitters, lifeguards, teachers, bosses, love interests, friends.

Searching for and finding Ruth uncovered so many things for me in becoming more aware of myself. The search process alone gave me confidence and a yearning to live my life large. The trip I'd made to Southern California introduced me to the beauty of that area — from the beautiful blue Pacific to the manicured landscapes decorated with foliage, to the natural terrain of the desert sage-covered mountains surrounding the coastline, I loved it all. I was riding so high from the accomplishment of finding my birth mother, and more than likely finding my birth father, I was filled with the confidence to entertain moving there.

As a single 25-year-old working in advertising, I could see no reason not to embark on this adventure. Another woman in my office, Lisa, was also considering a move to Southern California. We put our heads together and devised a plan. We were both determined and intentional about the move not only to be a wish, but an actuality.

Lisa and I became roommates and found jobs at the same advertising agency within the first week we arrived in sunny California. We were elated. The agency was worldwide, but our branch serviced only one high-powered client. It was a multimillion-dollar account for an automaker with full-service television, radio, catalog, print ads, and point-of-sale advertising campaigns. I took a demanding and fast-paced position in the broadcast department.

My job was to make sure each city and region's television stations were provided with the correct television commercials with the right rotation to air on the right day, at the right time. I was constantly in fight-or-flight mode. The never-ending threat of being unsuccessful meant the client could lose large amounts of money because television air space was so costly. Often my boss would call me after hours with an emergency scheduling change demanded by the client. To make this happen, I learned to build good relationships with all the national and regional television stations so they would be willing to accommodate our client's wishes. I've never felt so alive in a job, but I've also never been so exhausted and utterly depleted of energy from a job.

During my first week on the job, I met the director in charge of regional creative advertising. Our offices were close in proximity, and we would often run into each other in the hallway or the copy room. Rick was handsome, witty, and had a seductive nature about him. I fell for him almost immediately — never mind that he was 20 years older than me. He resembled a rugged "Marlboro man." Our flirting kept gaining energy and momentum until we were an item and soon moved in together. Lisa also began dating a man from our agency and they eventually married.

My new life in California was taking form. All seemed to

be well — I had a great job, a handsome live-in boyfriend and enough money to afford a beachfront rental house. I thought I'd designed the perfect escape from my painful childhood and now I could finally be me, my true self. I also thought that meeting my birth mother and potential birth father had "solved" all my adoption issues. While it was a big help, it didn't help me solve the puzzle that was my life.

The problem with finding my true self was that I couldn't remember who that even was. I didn't have a clue of how to get back there. Instead, I lived my life making decisions based on feelings and trying to outrun my unresolved grief and trauma.

After four years living together, Rick and I got married. I thought being married to him was proof that my life in California was successful. I needed to see him as a kind of romantic guru who would show me the way, and maybe even help me solve the Rubik's Cube mystery of my life.

Despite our earnings, we were living paycheck to paycheck and not saving anything. I idealized who Rick was, and he did a great job misrepresenting himself as a person of substance. I needed so badly to believe in him that I blatantly ignored all the red flags I encountered, including knowing that Rick's paycheck was being garnished to pay 15 years of back child support for one of his daughters. Rick insisted that it was his former wife's fault and that she was just being vengeful. He was also in trouble with the Internal Revenue Service for several years of unpaid taxes, and they had finally caught up to him and were threatening jail time.

Within a few years of our marriage, I sought the help of a therapist. I was seeking help with unresolved issues around being an adoptee and being an adult child of emotionally immature parents, as well as issues with my marriage. We didn't know at the time that it was unethical for the therapist to accept a client who was also her next-door neighbor.

My therapist set about fostering within me a deep emotional dependency upon her, even encouraging me to think of her as the loving mother I'd never had. In therapy sessions, I became confused early on because she kept telling me I was resisting and avoiding her attempts to help me. She told me of wanting me to have a breakthrough and that could only happen through trusting her explicitly. I expressed that I really was trying and that I wasn't familiar with the therapeutic process. After she openly showed me her frustration by reprimanding me for being resistant, I started altering my behavior and not listening to my inner voice. It reminded me of how I had to adopt people-pleasing traits with my parents to survive my childhood and teenage years. In much the same way, I was trying to please my therapist and show her how hard I was working. She'd then praise me and that would feel good. I didn't even mind when she began giving me hugs at the end of every session.

There's a powerful hormone that's released every time we give or receive a friendly or loving hug. It is the same hormone a mother and newborn experience right after childbirth. The hormone, oxytocin, has been called 'the cuddle hormone' or 'the love hormone' due to its association with pair bonding. Psychology articles have stated that oxytocin appears to help reinforce the early attachment between mothers and their infants, as well as the bonds between romantic partners. I had no way of knowing my psychologist was using her hugs, which I thought innocent at the time, as a way of grooming me. Having been relinquished by my birth mother (who never held me), and then having been adopted by a mother with no mothering instinct, meant that I was oxytocin deprived. This made me the proverbial sitting duck for this predator psychologist. Grooming is a tool she used to gain my trust, and ultimately manipulate that trust to gain advantages. My psychologist used other techniques to bond with me by using voice modulation, soothing tone, volume, and frequency of a hypnotic voice. There was also using the tool of pausing – ever so slightly, for too long of a time for effect and repeating key phrases that served to dominate, control, and confuse me. The effects were cumulative, and all played a part in shaping my psychological state of mind.

She slowly gained more control over me. Because I grew up in a household where I wasn't allowed to have boundaries, I was wide open to the manipulations of this skilled psychologist. The children of emotionally immature and problem-drinking parents also usually have low self-esteem and have been emotionally deprived. My parents had been too consumed by their own thoughts and feelings to tend to mine or my brother's. Although I recognized many red flags during my relationship with the therapist, I would rationalize them away by believing her when she told me I was resistant to surrendering to the therapeutic process. I accepted the gaslighting blame she placed on me that it must be my fault. And instead of guiding me to discover certain truths about myself and my upbringing, she used my unresolved trauma to specifically have an inappropriate sexual relationship with me. It was as if she seduced a child, given the vulnerable state I'd been intentionally and skillfully placed in by her. I trusted her to have my best interest at heart and to abide by the code of ethics she ascribed to as a doctor, The Hippocratic Oath, which says physicians will do no harm.

I also trusted the therapeutic process, which means the patient must become vulnerable in order to allow change to happen. I walked away from that psychologist in much worse condition than when entering therapy with her. She'd used my childhood trauma of both adoption and growing up in a dysfunctional home against me. Perhaps when I'd been a teenager, if I'd been given the permission to have my own feelings without serious repercussions, I would've been more in alignment with myself, others, and the world around me. Maybe it wouldn't have taken me as long to recognize that this exploitative therapist was getting her needs met instead of mine.

I had sought out counseling not only for adoption trauma, but also for marital issues. This exploitative therapist did nothing to help us with our marriage. In fact, we came very close to divorcing after the wedge she caused between us. Rick and I had plenty wrong in our marriage, but the therapist's motivation was to break us apart since she wanted me for herself.

I had given her a key one time when she offered to feed our cat when we were away. She called me at work one day and announced that she'd done what she knew I was not strong enough to do: she had moved my personal belongings into her house, right next door to Rick's and mine. She did this without my knowledge or consent. This audacious act of hers brought me to an extremely fragile, confused state rendering me almost paralyzed to have agency over my own life. I had become distorted by this therapist, somehow thinking she was what I needed to survive. I finally began to recognize she was manipulating me by emotionally handicapping me and basically making me her prisoner.

After I was able to break away from the almost hypnotic grip of this psychologist, I felt I had no other place to go. So, I chose to go back to my marriage with Rick. It was a slow healing process for me to deal with the awful aftermath of what my therapist had done to me, and to Rick. Although he was not the best partner for me, he was my advocate during the time it took for me to understand what the therapist had done. The awareness brought me to knowing that I couldn't allow her to do to others what she'd done to me.

We reported her to the state licensing boards and filed a lawsuit. I don't regret taking that action even though her attorney and the mediator re-traumatized me by trying to make it appear all my fault. Her attorney claimed I had orchestrated the entire event to "conquer the therapist." I now know that the responsibility for holding the therapeutic boundaries in place was solely hers and that most exploitative therapists use this kind of "responsibility role reversal" as their defense. During the trial, she was defended by her attorney whose sole objective was to win the case however necessary so as to save her malpractice insurance company thousands of dollars. This woman had turned my innermost thoughts and trauma against me and had sent me to a very dark place that I almost didn't return from.

Almost immediately after Rick and I had reconciled, I became pregnant. I had never been happier in all my life to find out that I was going to have a baby. Feeling life within me was an ineffable experience unlike any I'd ever had. The relationship between me and my unborn child was already forming, and it was healing me in ways I never thought possible. Rick and I were both solely focused on the pregnancy. This helped us begin to heal from the harm of the psychologist and it also put our troubled marriage out of focus for the time being.

Another healing action I took was to complete Master's level course work in psychology for Marriage, Family, Child counseling. As I learned about the history of psychology, psychological dysfunctions, personality disorders, and regulating one's behavior, I started feeling confident in seeing clearly the egregious misconduct of my previous therapist. The program was a lifesaver in helping me to unravel and unpack the transgressions of the therapist and to begin making sense of my adoption and childhood traumas.

Two and a half years later, Rick and I were pregnant

again. I had never known the kind of love, joy, and beauty that my daughter and son gave me, and still give to me. They also gave my life meaning and a purpose to work on myself so I could be better for them. I tried hard to justify staying in my failed marriage for their sake, and held on for 12 difficult years.

However, when I learned that Rick didn't pay our taxes and lied about it, that tipped the scale. His sense of entitlement and inability to take responsibility became abundantly clear. My marriage to Rick ended when my children were 8 and 10, but I remained focused on loving and caring for them. I had created a fantasy out of who I thought Rick was and now I needed to leave my marriage to give my children safety and a solid home base.

My life in California unraveled and now I had my two young children to consider. My relationship with my parents had improved during the almost 20 years I'd been away and was in a hopeful state of repair now that I was an adult and I had taught them how to treat me. Staying in California was not possible due to the high cost of living, so I considered a move back to my hometown where my parents lived. It felt like such defeat after how hard I'd fought to become liberated from my childhood. I promised myself that if any behaviors or abuse like that from the past were to ensue, I would take my children and move elsewhere. However, it proved to be the best decision I could've made as a mother wanting a safe and happy place for my children to thrive. My parents treated my children with love and care and proved to be a stable base in their young lives and on into adulthood. I, in turn, found a new way to love and appreciate my parents. I am so very grateful for how much they loved my children. I learned how to start reconciling how things are seldom either all good, or all bad, including my marriage to Rick. The fact is, I do love my parents for so many things. I came to terms with knowing that my parents love me, but they had so many of their own issues they hadn't settled within themselves. This so often made their love hurt, instead of bringing comfort. I finally was able to see that their transgressions against me had nothing to do with me at all.

My children have given me the gift of feeling "home" for the first time in my life. I am so grateful for them and having the opportunity to watch them now creating their own lives. The three of us share a bond that is very reciprocal. While I've shown them the way many times, I would say they've both been the most influential teachers of my life.

# THE GUEST OF HONOR

*The greater a child's terror, and the earlier it is experienced, the harder it becomes to develop a strong and healthy sense of self.*

— Nathaniel Branden
PSYCHOTHERAPIST AND WRITER

I n my favorite meditative state, I am in my canoe, floating down the river in the canyon surrounded by the tall green mountains. I lean forward in the bow of the vessel looking towards the water in front of me. My heart feels as though it is opening to the slow parting of the waters as my canoe glides steadily forward toward new spaces. New possibilities. It's an unfamiliar feeling but intoxicating to think of saying "yes!" to life. The feeling of being inextricably linked to the universal pattern of order, disorder, and reorder. It seems we all must go through this pattern of death and rebirth, again, and again, to get to the other side. Fear has no place for me in this moment.

And then I was brought back to my surroundings at The Gathering Place as I heard a silvery voice say, *"Can you see me?"*

I looked around to try to find where the voice had come from. I was becoming aware of not being alone.

Again, I hear, *"Can you see me? I am here."*

The voice sounded closer now. Almost right beside me. I stood to have a seat in the swing. Swaying slowly along with the breeze, I scanned my surroundings in hopes of seeing whoever was speaking. I had to listen closely. I was afraid I might miss any words spoken next. But I heard nothing. Only the light wind and the leaves rustling in the big old oak tree. I decided to answer that which I couldn't see.

"Hello? Is anyone there?" I asked hesitantly in a voice that was almost a whisper.

In my head, I was scanning the list of everyone invited to join me at The Gathering Place. They included all my parts who needed to know they were welcome and that they're all treasured and loved. I may have abandoned each of these parts at times throughout my life, but I was ready to embrace them all. I'd reunited with Tabitha, Lauren, Kate, and Mia. Each one of them were valued and necessary. My plan was not only to tell them I'll never leave them again, but to *show* them. Integrating all my wounded parts to become whole was my goal. If I could make them feel safe, this was key to bringing them home. I felt at least four of them there with me— and now, one more as I sat on the swing under the big old oak tree.

I spoke into the air again, "Hello? Who's there?" I was eager to meet my next guest.

*"They call me Baby Girl Ridgefort,"* said the voice in a light, yet clear tone. *"It means Dweller of the Stronghold."*

I calmed myself. My heart was trying to regulate itself from the understanding of knowing who this presence was. For some reason I had not thought to invite this part. So, it seemed that my unconscious must have. Until that moment it had not occurred to me that she, almost more than anyone, belonged there. In fact, she should be the guest of honor. While she was the youngest, she was also the one who had endured and suffered the original wound, the primal wound of being separated so young from everything she'd ever known. This was the trauma that was remembered in her (my) body, but not recalled in conscious memory. This infant had been given an impossible conundrum that would be hers to try and solve for the rest of her life.

"I'm so happy you're here," I said as I placed a hand over my expanding heart space. I was feeling a warmth envelope me that encouraged me to welcome her even more. "I've missed you so much. It was so brave of you to come," I spoke as I smiled and wept at the same time.

*"Can you please help me? I'm lost and need you to grab hold of me."*

"Yes! Of course, I will!" I wanted to help her in any way I could.

*"I need to feel you tether me to Earth. Can you please be the glue that I need in order to survive and thrive?"*

I immediately flashed on how I often describe my feelings of adoption to be like floating unclaimed in space. It's such a lonely and scary feeling of being lost. And of being *untethered*.

I continued, "What do you need from me? What do you need from me right *now?*"

The small voice said, *"Can you please hold me? I need to feel your skin against mine."*

Closing my eyes, I responded to the lyrical, sweet voice of the one who had been named Baby Girl at birth. I imagined her clear blue eyes staring into mine as I placed her in my arms for a soft, yet firm embrace. As I held her so very close, I felt safe and connected to her in the most surreal way. I'd never wanted anything so much than to fall into her gravity. It was as if the lines became blurred between who she was, and who I was. I felt an energy of fusion between her past, present, and future. All of these magical things happened as I breathed in her sweet, subtle scent of the top of her head knowing that this is the intoxicated feeling of being completely connected with another.

Years earlier, after the discovery of my birth name, I had researched the meaning of the surname "Ridgefort." Fort means "strong," and comes from Latin. Ridge means a high raised form providing protection for everything (or everyone) behind it. Even though Ridgefort was a fictitious name made up by my birth mother to protect her anonymity, as I held this baby girl at The Gathering Place, I thought the name perfectly described her present and future resilience and tenacity.

"Can you share with me where you've been; what you've seen?" I asked her quietly as I rocked her against my chest, and we sat in the swing.

My first conscious memory came to mind of being in a semi-dark room in my pale, yellow crib. At two and a half years old, I remember feeling a heavy sense of loneliness and wondering where *anyone* was. I would watch the moonlight from my window shining through the slates of my crib railings casting shafts of light in a neat row across my bedroom floor. Time would pass as I'd watch the beams move slowly from one side of the room to the other. Little did I know I'd discovered the age-old complex idea of how to measure the passage of time. As if I were measuring time by the moonbeams that were moving across my floor rather than watching a sundial, or a sandglass timer, or being able to read a clock.

Then I heard her speak, *"In the beginning, everything I'd ever known was there with me, and in the next moment, it was not. I felt utterly alone. Suddenly I no longer felt the familiar warmth that had enveloped me, heard the reassuring steady pulsing flowing sounds of life, experienced the sensations of vibrating motion, or the familiar voice that had always comforted me. I kept waiting for "home" to reappear. My home was warm and safe and was everything I'd ever known. But it never did reappear. The grief and sadness I felt of suffering this loss was sharp, cold, and unrelenting. Instead, I was falling, falling, falling and had no glue to help me know where I was in space or time. I was so lost and scared. Even with my senses sharpened and on high alert, still, all I felt was so lost and scared."*

Her words landed right in the center of my heart. Lightly stroking her tiny head, I said, "I didn't know how to be there with you then, but I'm here now. Thank you so much for sharing that part of you with me. I see you. You exist. Life wants you, and I want you." Baby Girl had just given me the ineffable gift of putting into language a description of our original, primal wound.

I felt an urge to ask her about the stolen notes that documented her as being a "sober, observant, non-crying infant" who was not interested in eating. Or ask her why the caseworker notes stated she was an unsmiling baby. I took a deep breath and exhaled. At that moment, I realized I didn't need to ask her these questions. I already knew the answers. She had described to me the anguishing feelings of loss she'd endured. Baby Girl had been in shock. Now, as I held her safely in my arms, I could only feel a kind of love that transcends space and time. Feeling this love was like being fully known and loved and seen for what I am, and reciprocating this love back to her. I looked down and saw she had drifted to sleep while we were holding each other and were sitting in the swing firmly attached to the big old oak tree.

# THE LONELIEST NIGHT EVER

*I can be changed by what happens to me, but I refuse to be reduced by it.*

— MAYA ANGELOU
AMERICAN POET,
CIVIL RIGHTS ACTIVIST, AUTHOR

The year was 1981 and it was 2:00 a.m. I was walking alone in the dark and deafening silence along the railroad tracks which I was praying would lead me back to my college dorm room on the other side of town. I just kept walking with the only sound of the night being my feet crunching the white gravel that lined the tracks. My panic was rising exponentially — I was not at all certain I was going in the right direction. The only lights I saw were distant through the tall trees and only enough that I could somewhat make out a building or two. That part of my college town was completely unfamiliar to me. I *did* consider veering from the isolated train tracks to go to a far-off store, but I was sure they would be closed. I don't think I have ever felt as utterly alone as I did that night.

It was spring semester my freshman year and my date and I attended an "Aloha" themed fraternity party. Everyone was wearing loud Hawaiian shirts, shorts or skirts, and several brightly colored plastic leis. Spring fever was definitely in the air at the university and other parties were going on all over town. The party was off campus at a local community Moose Lodge that the fraternity had rented for the night. My brother was an upperclassman member of the same fraternity and was there with his date somewhere. I had seen him briefly when we first arrived, but not after that. The main party was gathered in the dining hall where the music was loud, and everyone was dancing, singing, and drinking keg beer, spiked punch, or some other mixed drink. Kids were drunkenly jumping up and down and belting out the lyrics to Diana Ross's, *Ain't no mountain high enough, ain't no valley low enough, ain't no river wide enough, to keep me from getting to you, baby.* The partygoers seemed to know every word and would howl with laughter after completing each verse. The group beside us was especially out of control with the girls precariously perched on top of their date's shoulders. One of them kicked my red Solo cup of beer right out of my hand.

"Hey! Cut it out!" My date said, raising his arms over his head with a whoosh. My date was a boy I barely knew named Tommy. He was a freshman, too.

Within moments, Tommy had replaced the cup of beer in my hand and insistently led me away from the party into a smaller room and closed the door behind us.

"Why are we leaving the party?" I asked but was secretly pleased to be getting away from the drunken crowd. Flattered by his attention and happy to be his date, I went with him willingly.

"Oh, it's much nicer here away from those crazies! Here,

let me get you another drink. I'll mix you one with some good stuff I bought on my own."

I had learned in high school how alcohol would often make me feel transformed into being more interesting, more social. Since I didn't trust that just being myself was a good thing, I most often relied on alcohol to "make me better." The expectation of drinking large quantities of alcohol at college seemed a foregone conclusion accepted by everyone. As an undiagnosed people-pleaser at the time, I didn't even know I had the right to choose not to drink. Or that just being me was actually *good enough*.

The little room was crowded with a lot of furniture and looked like a storage room. Tommy had brought his own music and was blaring it to drown out the main party. He handed me the new mixed drink, but I was already feeling dizzy and disoriented. He led me over to a couch and began kissing me. His kisses were gentle at first but then changed to being more insistent. The room was spinning a little for me and I suddenly no longer wanted to be sitting on the couch with him. I started to feel pressured and groped— and not allowed to even take a breath from the sloppy kissing he was making me endure. I felt a chill in my body signaling to me that things were getting out of hand, and that I was possibly in trouble.

No one had ever prepared me for a situation like this or told me that I have every right to refuse an unwanted sexual advance. The attitudes I'd adopted from childhood led to feeling like I didn't have the right to refuse Tommy's advances. I grew up not knowing or understanding what boundaries were, or that I had a right to even set them.

A little too late, I realized that Tommy wasn't concerned with my comfort and that he had different ideas about what would happen next. The music was so loud that I doubted anyone could hear me frantically yelling for him to "stop" when he was raising my short jean skirt and was on top of me pressing me down onto the couch. I resisted and tried to struggle against him, but Tommy wasn't listening. Panicked, I began trying my best to maneuver myself out from underneath him. My physical endurance ran out and I was pinned into place by Tommy's much larger frame. I felt such shame and defeat as I succumbed to his will. I literally had no strength left to fight him off. It gave me no comfort knowing my brother, Tim, was somewhere at that same party since he was obviously not keeping tabs on me. I was sobbing and begging Tommy to please stop. And then he did. He suddenly felt like deadweight on top of me.

I smelled the alcohol on his breath as he removed himself and then he had the audacity to ask me, "What's wrong with you? Why are you crying?"

Where was my big brother, Tim? Why was I not screaming at the top of my lungs? Nothing was making any sense to me. I frantically gathered my things and started to leave. My date (rapist) offered to take me home, but I categorically refused. As I burst through the closed door where Tommy had led me, I'd felt everyone had stopped to stare at me as I fled the party. I wondered; did they all know? Did they see me looking disheveled and in obvious distress? Once I was out in the night air of the parking lot, only then did I think about how I would actually get home.

The music was still booming from the party inside the small lodge, and I could see partygoers dancing and screaming through some of the open widows. *I can't get no satisfaction* by Mick Jagger and The Rolling Stones was blasting. I was freezing in my short-sleeved Hawaiian shirt and skirt and sobbing with mascara running down my cheeks as I looked around to get my bearings. The contrast between the raging party inside and the quiet of the night air in the parking lot was stark. I was very sober by then. I saw a set of railroad tracks that seemed to be heading north, where I thought my dorm was located. I didn't really know anything for sure, but it seemed like the next best thing to do. I kept telling myself to just move away from the party in hopes it would be in the right direction.

Then I began the loneliest, longest three mile walk I've ever taken to get home in the chilly early morning air. It never occurred to me to call campus police and report that I'd just been raped. This was before cell phones, so I was out there walking the tracks silently. I had morbid thoughts of how ironic it would be if I were to get killed as I walked out there in the black night with no one around. I just kept walking in shock over how disgusted and horrified I was by what had just happened.

My skin, my hair, my hands, all of me, felt as if they were no longer mine. The smell of Tommy's Polo cologne still clung to my clothes and skin and was pungent in my nostrils. I longed for a hot shower to wash him off me and try to forget he existed. I don't think I've ever felt uglier than I did that spring night. I remember thinking, maybe after a shower I'll feel as though my body would be my own again? Feelings of being lost crashed around me, throwing me into a paradoxical state of being nowhere yet trying to frantically get somewhere. Each step I took threw me off kilter since the loose gravel on the tracks made walking in my sandals precarious. Part of me wished I'd just let Tommy take me home, but the other part knew I never wanted him anywhere near me ever again. The rhythmic act of walking along that linear railroad track helped me regulate. I was trying to make sense of Tommy's unabashed abuse of me and was using my anger-infused adrenaline to walk myself home.

In the days, weeks, and months to come, I was asked why I adamantly no longer wanted to be affiliated with the Lil' Sister program of the fraternity that had held the party. Since I had a brother in the fraternity, I was an honorary member. I told a few people that I'd been raped, including Tommy who had come over shortly after that night to see why I was so upset. He argued with me and claimed no responsibility. The year was 1981, a time before we, as a society, had become aware of listening to the victim of a sex crime. This scenario was also an example of me as a young woman not knowing my own worth. I knew no better than to bury the event in my mind and to "just get on with things."

I didn't remember being raped by Tommy until I was pulling weeds in my garden just a few years ago. I had recently entered sobriety and was beginning to reconcile all the issues I'd been running from for so long. It was a beautiful chilly spring morning, and I was putting my hands in the dirt and marveling at the new growth. The somatic experience of beautifying my garden had given my body permission to recall the experience to finally process the trauma. After I shared this repressed memory with my trusted counselor, I was able to feel safe enough to recall the entire memory — and others, too. All my wounded parts began to wake up and help me begin deconstructing the false self I'd built to survive my youth. It was all held together by the unspoken family message of "Don't talk. Don't trust. Don't feel." This construct trained me to think that I didn't deserve to have a voice. These are the stone walls of someone who is in prison, which I am happy to say, no longer apply to me.

Years later, I returned to my college town to see the Moose Lodge again where the fraternity party had taken place. I stood in the parking lot and looked at the exit door where I had fled to safety that night long ago. Imagining I could still hear the roar of the party going on inside, I remembered and honored the 19-year-old who had tried to control a situation that was out of her control. As I walked to the back side of the building, I also found the isolated railroad tracks that led me north to get back home.

# A NIGHTMARE FELT IN MY GUT

*Absence is a house so vast that inside you will pass through its walls and hang pictures on the air.*

— Pablo Neruda
Chilean poet-diplomat and politician,
Nobel Prize for Literature 1971

I recently had a nightmare. It was about receiving a phone call from my parents who sounded angry saying, "Get over here now!"

Then in my dream saying, "What's happened? Is everything OK?" There had been a series of falls and accidents over the last five years. They were now 92 and 87 years old. I knew some of the nurses at the emergency room by name since I'd brought them in separately on many occasions.

My father said, "You know what you've done! Get over here now!" He bellowed.

In my dream my blood curdled, and my gut wrenched. What had I done? This scenario was reminiscent of similar events happening throughout my life.

I had a high school friend whose household was the one

where kids would gravitate. Her mom was the assistant to the principal of our high school and was known and loved by all. My friend had an older sister and brother who were also friendly and fun to be around. I liked being with this family who didn't have screaming arguments and seemed to treat each other with love and respect. I would often go to church with them and hear messages of hope that really appealed to me. I didn't understand it then, but I was struggling with depression over needing to choose between being me or being the person my parents were demanding me to be. It was causing an existential split and angst within me. Both options represented a kind of death to me. Either I kill my true self, or kill the false self, the one that I'd become so they'd accept me.

One Wednesday night at church with my friend's family, the minister asked whether anyone wanted to be baptized. I had been exposed to all the promises I'd read about in the New Testament and wanted to accept Jesus into my life. I decided to accept the invitation. I felt elated by having made this gesture of faith to be baptized and was filled with new hope and promise. As if I could trust in a God who understood my heartache and my feelings of not belonging.

When I arrived home and entered the door of my home that night, I was met by my irate parents who somehow already knew of my experience of the night. How, though, I asked myself? That was less than an hour ago. How would they know? Who told them? My elation of having been baptized and made new in the eyes of God had dissolved by then into massive amounts of shame. They said things to me like, "You've shamed our family with you making a spectacle of yourself!" And "How ungrateful can you be? You were already christened in *our* church, you silly thing!"

They grounded me and forbade me to spend any time

with my friend or her family whom they said had clearly corrupted me with their religious views.

In the dream, my panic and fear were as real as when I was 15 years old and had been "busted" for being baptized. Or, just like when my mother's sister had told my mom that I had confessed to her that I had searched and found my birth parents. My parents had always told me that I'd be disowned if I ever searched. They didn't quite disown me, but they didn't speak to me for three anguishing years. My parents had always been quick to be punitive and unforgiving. Being treated this way would be difficult for most people, but as an adoptee whose worst fear is abandonment, it's terrifying.

I can see myself in my nightmare rushing to my parent's home at their demand. Upon entering the door to their home, they say, "We know what you did!"

Feeling like a pillar of stone I managed to ask, "Have I done it now? Have I finally done the deed that will make you leave me forever?"

In that moment of my dream, I realize that this is a process that I have repeated all my life as an adoptee. Always pushing people away, or holding them too close, or testing them to see if this will be the final straw that will make them leave me for good. Just like my birth mother Ruth left me. Leaving me after my birth and being OK with handing me to strangers. Forever. And really, many times in my past, I've always pushed my own self away. Telling myself that I don't deserve any better.

After my punishment for my crime of being baptized ended, my "acting out" phase began while still in high school. I changed my crowd. This time I chose the drinking crowd. And then drinking, going to parties, and dating boys who did the same all went together. Bad choices seemed to happen after too many drinks. At least it was in my case with going a little too far in most everything.

One night, coming home from a party driving drunk, I completely took my eyes off the road. I was shocked when I realized I'd driven my car into a ditch. It had rained recently and the mud from my tires splattered all over my car, even up onto the roof. Petrified of pulling up in my driveway with my car in that condition, I decided to stop by my boyfriend's house and hose it off. I didn't even ring the doorbell to ask if this was OK. It was fruitless anyway. The mud remained and I went home to the punishment that would surely await me. I was grounded for weeks, but the real punishment was my parent's all too familiar anguishing silent treatment.

This anguish, this nightmare, is why The Gathering Place holds so much importance and life-giving promise to me. I am making amends to myself for unknowingly abandoning myself so many times. In contrast, I am now choosing to be intentional about being present in my own life. As if I were learning to truly breathe again and regulate my emotions even though I was never shown how by those who were to take care of me. The Gathering Place represents an act of kindness of me holding space for me, in my own heart.

# FACING THE PAST

*To forgive is to grieve for what happened, for what didn't happen—
and to give up the need for a different past.*

— DR. EDITH EVA EGER
HUNGARIAN-AMERICAN PSYCHOLOGIST,
POST-TRAUMATIC STRESS TREATMENT,
AUTHOR, HOLOCAUST SURVIVOR

I was anxious to see who would show up next to The
Gathering Place. I took my usual spot in the swing and
gazed out over the green hills. The sky was ominous with
darker clouds moving in from the west. It smelled like rain.
The wind was blowing a little more insistently than the usual
light breeze, so I zipped up my jacket a little higher to ward
off a chill.

"Hey, I'm here." I heard someone say gruffly from the
other side of the tree. I spotted her and saw a young girl of
11 or 12 years old. Her long hair parted down the middle
hung over her face as if she were trying to hide. She wore
jeans and a tee shirt and was barefoot.

"Hi," I answered. "Welcome. What's your name?"

My new guest answered, "You don't care what my name is! You're just like all the rest that leave me alone without any thought. Did you ever think I might be lonely? Scared? Did you ever think I might need some fucking help?!" She almost spit out each word. After a pause, she said in a little calmer voice, "I'm Justice. My name is Justice."

I took a pause. I looked her in the eye and nodded in a gesture I hoped she would understand meant that I was listening. "I can't argue with that." I slowly stood from the swing and sat on the soft ground. I patted the grass next to me, inviting her to sit. She reluctantly moved one step closer and plopped to the ground.

"Do you want to talk about it?" I relaxed my body hoping to show her I was ready to talk it *all* through. I was ready to talk about whatever she needed to, without any judgement.

"Oh sure, I've fallen for that before. I've been told to say what's on my mind only to be slapped for it. How great is that?" she said facetiously. "Just a few months ago, I wrote a letter to my mom telling her of my feelings about growing up and stuff. I told her I was confused and that I didn't mean to be shutting her out.

It's just that I've been feeling weird – kinda moody all the time. I was trying to tell her I was sorry if I was acting strange."

I kept listening as Justice talked more. Things just started spilling out.

"After she was done reading the letter, she freakin' *laughed* at me first, and then started yelling. I got really scared. I always do when she gets like that. I couldn't understand what I'd done wrong. And then I got so angry. I kept telling myself to *never, ever*, be open with her again. How could I be so stupid to have trusted her? Didn't I know by now not to do that? Sometimes I really hate myself for being *so* stupid!"

Justice yanked a handful of grass, throwing it up into the light wind.

I immediately flashed to a memory of when my parents had moved us to a new city when I was the same age as Justice. It was an agonizing move. I had to leave a school, friends, and a neighborhood I loved. Things got much worse for me when my parents didn't get involved with my new school or pay any attention to the class I was placed in. This school placed higher academically achieving students away from lower achieving ones. I was placed in the next-to-lowest achieving level. I didn't know how this could have happened since I came to my new school with straight A's. After I told my mom, she said "they must have a reason for it. We don't want to tell them how to do their job." I was devastated. And I developed what I've always referred to as my "stupidity complex."

"What else, Justice? Tell me more." I knew how much she needed to get everything out. She needed to be given the opportunity to vent the anger she'd been having to stuff down deep in her soul for such a long time. It was painful, but these things needed to be spoken.

"They drink a lot. Every night. I hate hearing how my dad insistently shakes his bourbon glass, making the ice rattle against the glass loudly. *Shake, shake, shake.* It's like my insides rattle right along with it. I swear I can tell the type of mood he's in just by how hard he shakes his bourbon glass. Then he goes and pours another.

They're always fighting, slapping, and cussing at each other. One time dad shoved my mom and she hit the dishwasher and fell to the ground. They yell such awful things to each other. And then I get even more scared cuz that's when they turn on my brother and me. It doesn't matter if we've done anything wrong or not. We're made to sit at our kitchen table for hours hearing how awful we are. Once in a while, either Tim or I will pop off and say something we shouldn't, and we'll get hit really hard for it. We don't do that often. I hate my parents when they do this. I really feel like dying."

She took a reflective pause while looking out over the green hills. "I don't know what to do when they come to me, each one of them, and tell me they're divorcing the other one, you know? When they fight, they try to get me on their side and want to hear me support them. 'You know your father's an alcoholic and I'm going to take you kids in the morning and we're going to live with my mother,' my mom says a lot. And the scary thing is, I can't agree with anything they say about the other because after they make up, I'll be in trouble for anything I say! My friend's mom says this is called being put in a 'double-bind.' All I know is that it makes me feel like throwing up!"

Justice looked at me and then quickly looked away. She spoke next as she looked again out over the hills, saying, "There's something else." She cleared her throat. "I know my dad didn't mean to. I think he forgot who I was when he came home drunk a few times." Justice seemed unable to go on to explain.

I asked Justice to take a few breaths. "Take your time. I'm here for you and we can hang all day long, if that's what you'd like. I've asked you here to show you how much you matter to me. I want to *help*." I spoke these words as I felt my energy rising all the way from my toes, radiating through my body, all in wanting Justice to hear my words and believe.

"My dad ... sometimes gets a strange look in his eyes ... and sounds really drunk, you know, slurring his words and all." She paused to clear her throat again.

"He kissed me, and I could smell the alcohol on his breath. Then ... then he ... he put his tongue in my mouth and left it there." Justice put her face in her hands and sobbed.

135

Through her hand covered face she continued, "And I didn't shove him away! I was too afraid!"

I allowed us both to just be in the moment. I wanted to give us space in our togetherness, and in our remembering. After the needed silence I spoke, "What were you feeling when this happened, Justice?"

"I felt frozen to do anything! I was just so certain he didn't know what he was doing. We never mentioned or talked about it afterward. It's like we pretended it never happened. And it did happen more than once. I felt so much shame. It would have been tons worse to tell on him," Justice said.

I rephrased my question, "What are you feeling right now, Justice?"

"I'm so *fucking mad* he did that to me! I mean, what the hell? What kind of father does that?! How could he have not known what he was doing?" She was crying again and pounding the ground with her fist as she grabbed a small twig and broke it into little pieces.

"Justice, do you know you aren't to blame for what your father did?" I went on, "Do you know that you don't have to make excuses for him? He's an adult. He knew what he was doing, and he counted on the fact that you wouldn't say anything."

She hung her head and slumped her shoulders. Justice said in a whisper, "My mother is already so jealous. I prayed she wouldn't find out. She acts like I'm the other woman in the house most of the time. I feel awkward even living there. Like I'm not really wanted. But then at other times, all she says is that 'I'm the light of her life!' She says one thing but acts another. It's so confusing!"

I nodded my head in agreement. I remembered how I felt so apologetic for taking up space in my childhood home. Almost as if it were my own fault for having been adopted and them needing to take me as a substitute for their inability to have biological children. Maybe that was it. Maybe my brother and I were just too foreign for my mother to be able to accept as her own. Never attaching or becoming attuned with us since the very beginning.

I wanted to share with Justice that this situation, and so much more, were not hers to own or to hold. And, that our parent's choices, behaviors, and feelings of inadequacy were all their responsibility and not to be dumped upon their innocent children. If I'd known that then, I wouldn't have carried and internalized such a heavy impossible burden of assuming responsibility for them. You can always ask the question of what trauma happened to them that shaped them that way, but I feel, at the end of the day, each of us has a personal responsibility to do our own interior work and not remain unevolved. This kind of generational trauma is insidious and just keeps getting repeated. I expected more from my parents. I do not think they did the best they could with what they were given. While I do have a very complicated love for them, and am constantly forgiving them, I simply can not say that they did anywhere close to their best for me or for my brother.

I sat thinking of what tools I could offer Justice to help her combat her difficult situation. And then several ideas came to mind. All were in the vein of somatic techniques aimed at relieving the symptoms of post-traumatic stress through bodily experiences. Dr. Bessel van der Kolk, in his book *The Body Keeps the Score*, states that yoga, journaling, walking, singing, art, and even kickboxing, can help us process and release trauma. Throughout my life I've found all these modalities to be helpful and didn't even know I was giving myself therapy!

"Hey, what do you feel when you sing?" I was hoping to

lead Justice to see that she, too, does many of these somatic expressions to feel better.

"I don't know," she paused for a moment, still looking at the ground. "I like hearing my voice in my head. Sometimes I like going into the garage to sing cuz it's all echoey and stuff in there."

"Oh, I like that idea! That sounds like fun. Maybe kinda like singing into a microphone?" I asked.

"Yeah, I'm in a lot of singing contests and have to learn songs in Italian. They're kinda tricky to sing so I like hearing my voice clearer so I can hit every note just right." I was pretty sure I saw her demeanor perk up as she talked about her singing practice.

"Very creative," I said. "Do you have any other interests or hobbies?"

"Funny," she said with a little frustrated chortle, "you would know! You're me, just a lot older."

"Ha-ha, yes — you're right. I just wanted you to recognize the things you do that help you in those tough times. Things *you* do for *you*." I was hoping I hadn't lost her by acting as if I didn't already know the answers to my own questions. She was quick and clever, and I wasn't going to be anything but transparent with her.

"Well, I'm a pretty good springboard diver. I practice a lot in the summers. It gets my mind off a lot of things."

"I know what you mean, Justice. Both of those activities helped us express ourselves in ways that others wouldn't allow us to. Something that really helps me now is cardio kickboxing. It allows me to kick and punch, and sometimes even growl, which helps me blow off a whole lot of steam!" She looked at me and leaned in just a little.

"Justice, your situation is a difficult one. *What happened to you mattered.*" I took in a long breath before going on. "But I'll tell you this; You have a spirit of tenacity and resilience. I want you to remember *that* in the many difficult and often anguishing moments you are and will be having. I'm here to help you, sweet girl! I know your pain and I'm here to tell you that you're *more* than worthy and that *you matter.* You matter — regardless." I drew her in, and she willingly let me hug her tight. I repeated softly, "You matter — regardless."

# FINDING STRENGTH THROUGH ORIGINAL PAIN

*Post-Traumatic Stress — It's a war within yourself that never goes away.*

— AUTHOR UNKNOWN
FROM *BURIED ABOVE GROUND* DOCUMENTARY 2017

Through loving my garden and watching it grow, I feel my *self* being nurtured at the same time. The front of my house faces north and gets full sun exposure. Taking advantage of this, I've planted hot purple Crepe Myrtles that are stunning when in bloom. I've also planted light pink, magenta and coral SunPatiens that love to soak up the hot summer sun.

One day I was immersed in tending my garden. My back was to my neighbor's house while I was bending down into my flowerbed to pull a weed and spread some mulch. My thoughts were far away, and I was not prepared for the angry bark of a big dog right behind me. I have an overdeveloped startle response that developed in my youth from my parent's unpredictable behaviors, so the sound of the dog sent my central nervous system instantly into complete unregulated panic. As I whirled around, I saw my next-door neighbor's unleashed giant standard poodle barking at me. It wouldn't have mattered whether he was leashed or not, my reaction would have been the same. My stress levels went from 0 to 60 in an instant. I went directly into fight or flight mode regardless of my neighbor telling me her dog wouldn't hurt a fly. Again, the part of my brain that could have received that information was shut down in that moment of red alert. At first, I stood paralyzed just staring at the loud barking dog that was lunging at me. Then I ran. I ran as fast as I could into the safety of my house. Only then could I identify my feelings of distress: shaking uncontrollably, sobbing, heart racing, sweating, all systems on alert. After the adrenaline lessened, I was left with crying episodes for the remainder of the day. Curious, I sat with myself searching for deeper meaning. And then it became clear to me what had happened. The angry barking, lunging dog had represented a scary, angry parent from my past where I was concerned for my safety. It was as if I had experienced this memory in real time and my defense mechanisms were fully activated for protection. I had come to recognize from other times that something similar had happened to me, that my brain had been hijacked by post-traumatic stress.

Just as other life situations have triggered my original trauma of biological separation, my dysfunctional upbringing can often do the same. I refuse to feel helpless over being hijacked in these ways though, instead, I've learned that practicing mindful awareness is key to bringing myself back to the here and now. In this way, I hope to be able to minimize these episodes and deactivate them with more ease and speed through practice.

During a recent therapy session with my EMDR counselor, Joanna, she guided me through a triggering event that would be upsetting to most, but there were deeper issues at play for me. It centered around the fact that my Bengal cat, a breed known for requiring a large amount of social engagement, often feels that the way to get my attention is to urinate on my bed. Ouch. A behavior I'm still hoping she'll outgrow, but until then, it's problematic! One night, just before dozing off to sleep, I lazily placed my laptop on the floor beside my bed. The next morning, I awoke to see my laptop glistening with wetness. After rushing to the nearest Apple store, it was confirmed that I had lost everything on my laptop due to the "liquid."

"Emma, I'd like you to hold the thought of what you were feeling when you realized your laptop couldn't be repaired," Joanna suggested.

Holding the EMDR pulsers in each hand — for bilateral brain stimulation — I took a deep breath and began to allow my brain to process. Joanna has created a lovely space in her therapy office that feels both safe and secure. It's a little amazing to me, given my background of having been exploited by a previous therapist, that I could indeed feel safe and allow myself to be vulnerable. But I do feel safe, and we have rapport and trust. After about 30 seconds, she checked in with me about what I was sensing.

"Helpless and feeling lost. The entire story I've been writing was on that laptop," I said.

"Tell me more about that lost feeling," Joanna gently encouraged and then turned the handheld pulsers back on for my hands to hold and stimulate my right and left side of my brain.

"It's like I can't breathe and I'm panicking. I feel like I will do anything to make this feeling go away. To not feel lost, desperate, or feel despair anymore. I feel like my survival depends upon it."

"OK, now I'd like you to concentrate on *that* feeling and let me know if anything comes up for you," Joanna said as she invited me to go deeper into exploring these feelings.

"I don't really care all that much about the laptop itself. It can be replaced. What I care about is losing my story which is contained on my laptop. That story is *me*. And if I lose the story, then I feel that I've lost *me* again. I've scratched and clawed my way to being able to discover and make sense of everything."

And then I hesitated with recognition, "I think the *loss* of this laptop is my original wound talking again!" I said to Joanna as I opened my eyes with this realization.

"Good! So, let's keep going with this and see where it takes you," Joanna said as I shut my eyes again to allow the process to continue. While I seldom draw a blank during an EMDR session, I sometimes worry about not being able to concentrate and stay on task. But I figure that would be important to know, too. That would undoubtedly mean something. So, I seldom stress over it too much. On this occasion, I was having no problem processing because I had just made solid connections with other similar "lost" moments.

"Oh my gosh! Something just occurred to me. This lost, lonely feeling also applies to when I walked the railroad tracks back in college to hopefully get home after being raped. Or even when I felt like I needed to escape to my brother's room at night in hopes of finding love and safety. And then all the sad songs I would play over and over on my little record player as a kid, or when I would cry uncontrollably over Disney movies with sad themes. This all makes so much sense!" My feelings at that moment were not of sadness but of joy to have had these insights. I continued with one more connection. It was my past relationship with alcohol.

"I also think I drank to try to outrun all my feelings of despair. Drinking helped to keep my feelings at bay and not deal with them. I remember having thoughts that I needed alcohol for my very survival. But alcohol freakin' lied to me! It wasn't my best friend comforting me! The drug tried to make me think I talked better, looked better, performed better, and that I was just better in all situations. The reality was that it was killing me. My relationship with alcohol almost killed me."

"Your brain is making these connections and letting you see things more clearly." Joanna paused before going on, "Also, didn't you write your story? Couldn't you write it again, if you had to?" She asked with eye contact that felt reassuring.

"Yes, so maybe I just need to trust myself and recognize that the story is inside me and can never be lost. I'd like to remember in those situations that I can be there for myself. Instead of abandoning myself."

"What other things would you say to yourself to help you regulate your emotions?" Joanna was smiling, and I wondered whether it was because she was enjoying watching me navigate myself out of turmoil.

"Trust that I wrote it before, and I can write it again. It's within me. And, while I was relinquished before, I don't need to re-abandon myself by experiencing this pain again, and again. This perceived loss has also made me realize just how important writing this book is to me."

And then she offered, "You might want to think about including this session in your book!"

These experiences have all taught me that what happened to me as an infant, and then in childhood and beyond, all mattered. The unresolved trauma that has been stored in my body and is operating just beneath the surface of my psyche, can be activated at any time. My *defense* is to know that my *desire to change* outweighs (and it most definitely does) my desire to stay the same.

# DNA DOES NOT LIE

*In the social jungle of human existence, there is no feeling of being alive without a sense of identity.*

— ERIK ERIKSON
GERMAN-AMERICAN PSYCHOLOGIST

One night I received a text from my daughter who was then 24 years old. She had just received her DNA test results from 23andMe and wanted to tell me something she found interesting.

"Mom, I think you should look at the email I sent you listing all kinds of close relatives that popped up on my DNA report," my daughter said.

"What?!" I couldn't understand what she had just said. "What do you mean?" I had certainly heard of Ancestry.com and 23andMe, but I hadn't really given it much thought. That may seem crazy, given how I was the sleuth of the 1980's and was all about discovering and uncovering all I could about my story!

I pulled up the email she had sent and saw names listed that were closely related to my daughter. After thinking about it, I said, "If these people are your 1st cousins, once removed, then that must mean they're my first cousins!"

To this day, I'm not sure why I hadn't thought to take a DNA test to find more biological relatives. Specifically, to have the answer of finally knowing whether James Adam Lehmann was my biological father or not. To be 100 percent sure. The only reason I can think of was that I was distracted by other life issues at the time. But the call from my daughter that night changed that in an instant. I was hot on yet another trail to discover the rest of my adoption story.

The first thing I had to do was order a kit from 23andMe. *Immediately.* I knew it could take at least a few days to receive in the mail, and then another six to eight weeks for my results to be determined. I used that waiting period to set about familiarizing myself with their website. I didn't quite understand how to navigate or make sense of all the different tabs, or what the content meant exactly. It took a little time, but it started to make sense. The feelings of being right on the precipice of finding out more about my story were so reminiscent of 34 years ago. My heart was beating wildly as I fell right back into my investigative skills of the past. Except now, I was using much more sophisticated means of finding my information. FaceBook became my new best friend. I stared at my daughter's list of relatives reported by 23andMe but didn't recognize any names. I knew that there was a possibility these DNA relatives could all be from her father's side, her paternal side. The closest relative that showed up for my daughter popped right up on FaceBook when I put her name in the search bar. Since there were a few people with her same name on FaceBook, I started clicking on her friend list to see friends or family members. After several failed attempts, I found the person I was looking for. I knew this because a person in her FaceBook friend list had the same last name as her and was also listed by 23andMe as a close relative. She was probably her daughter, I surmised after I looked up this person's picture and profile. So now I knew I'd found the right person on FaceBook that matched the same DNA relative of my daughter's. It was my task to find out *how* they were related to my daughter. And, if they were related to my daughter – were they also related to me?

After much anticipation and preoccupied thoughts, the DNA kit finally arrived in the mail. I couldn't spit in that tube fast enough. The only problem was that it's not that easy to produce the amount of saliva that's needed to fill the tube to the necessary marked line! It takes a while for your body to replenish to be able to produce more. Oh my gosh, that meant I had to practice patience again! After about 30 minutes of doing the process, I finally had the tube filled and placed it in the protective envelope provided to send it off in the mail. I knew I would need to wait more than a month for my results, so I returned to doing preliminary research based on certain assumptions I was making about who these people were that showed up on my daughter's report.

I started looking deeper into the "friend" list of the closest relative indicated on my daughter's 23andMe report. Scrolling through the long list, I was trying to find matches with the same last names. I found another one almost right away. It appeared to be the son of the closest relative. I had now identified three people who were on the DNA report.

"Dana! Look what I've found!" I called my daughter.

She was in her master's program in another city, but we kept in regular contact. I've always told her she's "my person," the one I go to before anyone else to share things with. She's unlike anyone I've ever known, really. The quiet confidence she possesses is that of a young wise old soul that has a seemingly endless capacity to love and stay connected.

I was ignited with the kind of excitement that I'd felt in my past with feeling as though a seismic change was about to take place. This was because in the FaceBook friend list of the closest DNA relative to my daughter, a surname had popped up. It hadn't shown in the DNA relative list, but it was showing up in the friend list. I felt I was on to something. I'd really grown addicted to that old feeling of being just about to bust a case wide open! I didn't have my own DNA results yet, so I still didn't know if these biological relatives were from my genetic pool, or Dana's father's.

"Dana, in the FaceBook friend list of a biological relative of yours I found a few people with the surname of *Lehmann!*" I then reminded her that the father listed on my original birth certificate is *James Adam Lehmann*.

"Mom, I admit that sounds encouraging, but Lehmann is a pretty common last name."

This is just one of the things I adore about my adult daughter. She always keeps me grounded and centered. When I tend to act before having all the information needed, she has taught me how to take a pause and be less reactionary. However, inside I was a ball of exploding energy and almost positive I was going to discover I'd been right all along about James Lehmann being my biological father.

I went down all kinds of rabbit holes alternating between FaceBook, Googling names of people, and using TruthFinder for double checking my findings. The most beneficial source was reading threads of conversations between people I suspected to be biological relatives and a definite family tree started appearing to me. There was one person I found specifically that appeared to be a family member and was a common denominator of most all the people I was researching.

I told my daughter, "I think I've researched as far as I can and need to wait for my own results."

"Yeah, that's when you'll know for sure if these are your

relatives, or dad's. How much longer, do you think?" Dana asked.

"They sent an email saying they were in the process of analyzing the sample. The waiting is excruciating!" I admitted.

It didn't take as long as 23andMe said it would. On Mother's Day morning, I found an email saying my results were in. There it was. That feeling of a dopamine hit again! I'd felt this same feeling of excitement throughout my many years of searching for my story. I thought I'd found everything I was ever going to find 34 years ago. Now I was finding out more than I'd ever anticipated. One thing that my previous reunion with my birth mom taught me was not to have any expectations. I found with Ruth, that while we tried to have a relationship, we just didn't have rapport with one another. There was no cosmic connection between us. I'll always be grateful to have met her, but I've found that my healing has come from within rather than from anything external. I was keeping this in mind, as I was possibly facing discovering these new biological relatives.

It was time for me to open the DNA results. The first thing I zoomed in on was that the report said that my daughter, Dana, was listed as my closest DNA relative. My heart was beating with joy over this obvious finding. I must admit, I had an irrational fear the report may say otherwise. I can't explain it, other than to say that it was fear-based. Fear of being told that my daughter wasn't really mine.

Maybe I'd dreamt the entire thing of giving birth to her (despite having documented it on video). I think the fear came from the wounded place in me that relinquishment caused, where I'm certain I'll lose anything I love. Seeing this proof on paper also made me feel entirely relevant, and that I exist. As an adoptee, feeling "real" has always been an issue. This was proof, though. Proof that I exist and that I gave birth to my daughter, and I have these DNA results to prove it. I'm not prohibited in any way to obtain this documentation by law or told that she was relinquished and was only named "Baby Girl." In the next few years, I would repeat this same process by having my son, Trevor, take a DNA test and then having the joy of seeing the positive test results once again.

In the next moments, I saw that all the assumptions I'd been holding onto ever since I'd viewed my daughter's results were correct. *Bam!* These people were *my* close relatives, as well. I again looked up the friend list of one of the cousins listed on my results and saw how many connections she had with people having the last name of *"Lehmann,"* the same last name as the father listed on my original birth certificate. A plan started forming in my head. In a déjà vu kind of way, I was again thinking through my next move.

# MAKING PEACE

*You're only truly free until you belong everywhere, nowhere, which is everywhere. The price is high and the reward is great.*

— MAYA ANGELOU
AMERICAN POET,
CIVIL RIGHTS ACTIVIST, AUTHOR

For the second time in my life, I was placing a phone call to a biological relative announcing to them of my existence. This time it was to a paternal cousin who would confirm that James Adam Lehmann was indeed my birth father. While James had not taken a DNA test himself, the proof was in all the relatives that *had* tested and matched with both me and my children. When I asked my cousin whether there was a Lehmann in the family named James, she confirmed immediately. My birth father had died only a few years before I found him for the second time. I'll never forget him looking me in the eyes 34 years ago and him saying, "I only put my name on your birth certificate to help a friend." A friend that he said he couldn't even remember her name. And, when he hugged me, he knew full well he was hugging his biological daughter for what would be the first and only time ever.

The Lehmann family has shown me kindness and has been welcoming. My cousin informed me on our first phone call that I have a younger half brother named David. Shortly after that phone call, I had the opportunity to meet him. Our reunion was sweet, informative, awkward, and a little messy. David grew up knowing nothing about me. He only learned of me when I emailed him telling him of my existence. He had a strained relationship with his father, James, and he shared that he had very few fond memories of him. It's early in our reunion and time will tell what path our sibling relationship will take. For me, my searching has always been about a journey to self, as opposed to finding one family to replace another. I do feel that I have room in my heart to accommodate loving both. I'm certain that the discovery of my amended biological lineage helped me in things like genetic mirroring and gaining feelings of being tethered to this world in a meaningful way. And I wouldn't want to skip over the ineffable feeling of seeing my unamended birth certificate for the first time. All these things played a big role in finding me and to begin to make sense of my world.

Now I'm at the point of my journey where even more is being revealed. There's a difference now though since my discoveries are happening internally versus externally. I'm exploring how I'm still me regardless of who my parents, or my birth parents were. I am me. I continue to try not allowing others to define me, and certainly not oppress me. This means I understand that the only person who can save me is me. As a person on this Earth, I feel I have a responsibility to do the necessary interior work that is crucial for my happiness as well as for those around me. It may not have the same thrill of the chase that my earlier search for my roots held but obtaining the awareness to do the unearthing of certain truths is just as much or more rewarding.

I've been invited by my recently found Lehmann first cousins to join them for a reunion in Flagstaff, Arizona. There might be 10 or 15 cousins in attendance. The idea of accepting the invitation floods me with a variety of conflicting emotions. They've obviously spent decades together with rich family history to be able to reminisce about, joke about, laugh about, cry about. And then there will be me – the "ghost cousin," who they know nothing about other than that I've lived in a kind of alternate reality separate from them. I would imagine that both my cousins and I will be partaking in a kind of salad bar of curiosity for one another. This leads me to again contemplate whether my full narrative has been revealed, or not. Each time I've had the thought of, "there, that's it. There's no more for me to discover about my adoption story," I've been pleasantly surprised. Even when the discovery has not been one that was easy to comprehend, like was the case with reading about my birth mother trying to abort me at seven months of pregnancy. However, if I've learned anything, it's that *life wants life* — it's just the way of things. It makes me sad to think that Ruth didn't ever seem to discover this to be true for her own life. I learned she died just this past summer, only a few weeks after my adoptive brother, Tim. While Ruth and I had not spoken in years ever since our short reunion that lasted only a few years, she's now left me in a whole new way.

# THE ADOPTION CONSTELLATION

*Happiness can exist only in acceptance.*

— GEORGE ORWELL
ENGLISH NOVELIST, ESSAYIST,
JOURNALIST AND CRITIC

I received a phone call early one morning. It happened to coincide with the middle of the Coronavirus pandemic.

"Hello?" I answered.

"Emma, this is Riley." I was surprised by this call from one of my brother's adult children. My system was immediately on alert because Riley never calls me. We've never had any kind of meaningful relationship, or have I had with Tim's other four adult children. This was primarily due to the long physical distance of where I lived and where my brother Tim's adult children lived and live. That's not the only reason though.

"I needed to call and tell you that my dad had a fatal heart attack early this morning," Riley said through tears.

"What?!" This was all I could think of to say. I was

suspended in time as I tried to make meaning of what Riley had just told me.

"Yes, he died on the way to the hospital. The paramedics were able to bring him back once briefly, but he died." Riley said. "My mom wanted me to call and tell you and she hopes you'll call nana and papa to let them know, too."

The more I thought about this news, the more I realized it was not that much of a surprise. Tim had suffered a smaller heart attack just two years earlier and had a stent inserted to help the blood flow to his heart. He had coronary heart disease. He was told by his doctor he must change his lifestyle immediately in order to prevent future heart attacks.

Tim did not change his lifestyle. He continued to smoke, drink, have poor nutrition, and seemed unable to manage the stress from his unresolved adverse childhood experiences, a volatile divorce from the mother of his five children, and a co-dependent relationship with one of his sons who shared his addictions.

After the phone call from Riley, I knew my next dreaded step must be to go to my parent's, who lived only two miles away from me, and deliver the news that their son had passed. My parents are in their late 80's and early 90's and my heart was breaking thinking of how I was going to share this news with them. The news that their child had passed before they did. I was barely able to wrap my own head and heart around absorbing the news. This was the brother that my mom and dad had promised me so long ago was going to be there for me after they had passed on.

The realities of the Coronavirus and the restrictions to travel made the planning of Tim's graveside services challenging. It was decided that only myself and my daughter, Dana, would fly to attend the service. Once there, we were joined by Tim's five adult children. Two of them lived with

Tim, and the other three had flown in for the service, and to be with their other siblings.

Dana and I did not receive a warm welcome from my brother's children. We made plans to go to their home right after we checked into our hotel. I had more or less invited ourselves over to see them and to be together as a family as family usually does after suffering a loss such as this. But instead of it feeling like being with family — it felt like being with five strangers who just sat there staring at us. We all had our masks on, and that made things a little more awkward, but it became clear that if there was going to be any communication, it was going to be up to me.

"I'm so sorry about all of this. I'm sorry for your loss," I said in hopes of learning more. "Can you tell me what happened?"

Silence. My brother's five adult children, all in their 30's, continued staring at the ground.

"Was he not feeling well that night?" I kept probing.

"He got up around 3:00 a.m. saying he wasn't feeling well," said the son who lived with Tim. He said he called the paramedics. "They got here, but dad had a heart attack while they were on the way to the hospital."

"And they were able to revive him once?" I asked.

"Yes. But not for long. He died before they even made it to the hospital," another of Tim's adult children said.

And that's all the conversation there was. I tried countless times to connect but never felt any reciprocity or received any condolences that I'd just lost my brother, and my daughter had lost an uncle. Dana and I were exhausted from the airport and flight and decided to end this "family" get together. We made plans to see them the next day at the cemetery where the graveside service was to be held.

"Mom, it's like they don't think of you as uncle Tim's real sister! I feel awkward even being here because of really not feeling welcome. I feel like they want us to leave," Dana expressed.

An all-too-familiar feeling had settled over me after having spent that short visit with my brother's adult children. I realized they didn't see me, or Dana, as "real" family. It's as though they were only tolerating our presence. The next day at the service I felt this even more to be true.

We had all decided to not have a clergy perform the service, instead, any one of us were welcome to speak on my brother's behalf. In the end, it was only my daughter, my brother's son-in-law, and myself who spoke. None of his adult children decided to do so. About 10 of my brothers' colleagues showed up to show their love and support. This meant so much to me. It revealed to me a whole new perspective on what kind of positive impact my brother had had on others.

I was so happy Dana had come with me — but I also felt awkward and unwelcome at my own brother's funeral. Tim's children all resembled him. All five were tall redheads with freckles, and fair skin. In contrast, Dana and I have brown hair, we are 5'3" tall, and have light olive skin.

It began to strike me, and even more in the months following the funeral, that just because a couple adopts a baby, claiming it as their own, does not mean that others in the family constellation feel the same conviction.

In my youth, there was no sense of ownership from anyone else in my family other than my parents. Grandparents, aunts, uncles, cousins — they all looked at my brother and me with leery sideway glances. They were told to accept us into the family as one of their own, but I now see there was a failed attempt to attach and truly accept us as anything other than foreign. We represented *the imposters that came from somewhere else*. And I see how this insidious frame of mind also kept my brother and me from feeling accepting of not only other family members, but each other as true brother and sister. No one in my family was prepared for the heavy psychological lifting that having adopted children requires in order for everyone in the family to thrive. It seems that grafting an adopted baby onto a family tree, family and parents must be prepared to lovingly tend to that child's unique needs. Otherwise, just as it is in nature, the chances of the grafting being incompatible can be the result of genetic differences between the grafted parts. An arborist knows that graft incompatibility, improper technique, or environmental conditions may cause graft failure resulting in general ill health of a tree, or a clean breaking off of a tree at the graft union. This may occur one, two, or many years after the graft is made. There are obvious parallels between this well-established fact in nature and in the practice of adoption.

Through my 12 step program I realize the need for me to be *willing* to have the *willingness* to accept my reality and to find forgiveness. Forgiveness for others and for myself. It really all comes down to my ability to lay things down. And not pick them back up again.

As I reconcile more and more of my life, I'm no longer held captive by feelings of ambiguous loss that my adoption caused. It's a trauma that's caused by suffering the kind of loss without any resolution and seems impossible to grieve properly. I will need to continue being aware of, accepting and reconciling these challenging ambiguous feelings of loss throughout my lifetime. Only then can joy and happiness exist within me.

# IN THE SPIRIT OF WHOLENESS

*Maturity is the ability to joyfully live in an imperfect world.*

— RICHARD ROHR
AMERICAN AUTHOR, SPIRITUAL WRITER,
AND FRANCISCAN FRIAR

I took a seat on the ground amongst all my "parts of self" at The Gathering Place. My heart space felt so full that it was opening and enlarging as if to create unlimited new growth. We were all sitting close in a circle on the soft grass under our big old oak tree. Next to me was little, sweet Tabitha. She was petting Miss Tabby Cat and placing the cat's fluffy tail up to her own lip like it was a mustache. This made us all laugh. Sitting on my other side was Mia holding one of the smooth river rocks from the stream she'd found along the bank. She was rubbing the palm-sized reddish golden rock in a calming, soothing way. Lauren, my 14-year-old self, was sitting with her legs crossed and smiling at her new friend, Tabitha. Lauren was even allowing herself to sneak a few chances to pet Tabby, who was now giving herself a luxurious bath. Kate, my 18-year-old self, was present and looking unusually relaxed. She rested back on one arm, with her legs extended long in front of her. Justice sat the farthest away, but directly across from me making eye contact easier. She needed more time. She was still trying to decipher whether she could trust that all of us were offering her a safe place to land. The good news was that she'd shown up. It was a start.

As I sat with myself and the others, I felt the joy of feeling Baby Girl's light breathing while I held the solid weight of her warm softness in my arms. Having this little one in my arms made our circle complete. I was in wonder of her incredibly magnificent deep blue eyes that helped me understand what love truly looks like. A love that keeps expanding right along with the ever-expanding universe. While my own eyes are green now, my daughter and my son had these same eyes. My gaze now locked onto Baby Girl's; no words were necessary for the intimate communication we were sharing.

I lifted my eyes and saw all my parts still forming a circle, but this time, it was as if they were all different colors of the spectrum. Both Tabitha and the baby were shades of blue watercolors, matched with yellows. Lauren and Kate shone with hues of greens, crimson reds, and hot purples. Mia was a rich reddish, golden amber shade that changed colors with the light. Justice showed up in a stimulating black and white checked pattern that revealed both her simplicity and her complexity. As a collection, they created a beautiful contrast of varying colors that magically all worked together as one.

# A NEW DAY

*Spare me perfection. Give me instead the wholeness that comes from embracing the full reality of who I am, just as I am.*

— DAVID G. BENNER
CANADIAN PSYCHOLOGIST,
AUTHOR "HUMAN BEING AND BECOMING"

I once heard God, The Holy Mystery, described as *the harmony of every harmony*. And, that the harmony of the universe is wholeness, not perfection; more specifically, it is wholeness that involves differentiation. This creates an auditory image so vivid for me of hearing absolute pure voices moving effortlessly into a five-part melodic harmony. These parts are all distinct and live only steps, and sometimes octaves apart, but all are needed to form the whole intricate harmonious piece. Without wholeness, we hear only noise of the various parts of ourselves, clanging together. Without differentiation, we hear only the pure sound of a single tone, but not its harmonics ... I've come to believe this about my own various parts of self, that they have differences, but each have purpose and meaning. They, too, can join in a beautifully wonderous way, like a mosaic of perfectly imperfect broken bits of colorful glass fitting together and transformed into art. I now know that there's power in "oneing"; integrating to become whole. Through grace and acceptance, I find myself moving closer towards flinging open the center of my being to the mysteries of what can be.

I've thought about how although I may have a clear mission in life, there has seldom been a clear path. My view has at times become distorted along the way and perhaps I've even become addicted to my own way of thinking without even knowing it. Most of us are, although we may not know it. Black and white thinking can certainly blind me from finding deeper degrees of clarity and identifying different shades of gray. Perhaps that's one of the reasons my symbolic Rubik's Cube has always felt so convoluted. I would never be able to make any significant results on this puzzle of frustration until I found my coherent and cohesive adoption narrative that spoke to my beginnings. One of the most important discoveries of all my searching has led me to understand that since my conception, I've been holding onto *what is not mine to hold.* I'm not responsible for anyone's actions but my own. And I would ask, how could I have become anything other than a fearful person with an overdeveloped sense of responsibility who would have troubled relationships, addictions that would be failed coping skills, and a host of other self-sabotaging behaviors? How could I have dealt with the on-going mental and physical abuse without developing complex PTSD?

It often feels to me, however, that it's because of my suffering that I've developed that fire in my belly. Instead of making my trauma and adaptations my prison, I'm making it my opportunity to transcend. It's through that suffering that I've learned the more I search for my authenticity and align with my true self, the more joyful I am. Paradoxically, to find my true self, I think I had to first walk through shadow. This self-awareness has helped me recognize the need to shed my old skin, and to do this *daily*. The result of not doing so leads me to repeating my old familiar maladaptive behaviors that only cause more pain. Instead, I now more often accept the reality that good and bad are interwoven, intertwined, and bumping up against each other.

I know that grace and generosity are not fair, by their very essence. Every morning when I am lucky enough to wake up, I have the chance to own this for myself. I now understand that the grace and love I receive is not due to anything I've done, or haven't done. It was a grand day when I finally said "yes, please!" to this gift that is given so freely. To make this happen, I first had to admit that I, too, qualify to receive it. Gone is my notion that somehow my wrongdoings are far worse than others and are unforgivable. Also gone is my erroneous belief that The Holy Mystery will deliver mercy and grace to all others — except to me. I'm thankful that this inclusivity means all are welcome and not just a chosen few. Coming into this awareness has cracked wide open my old perceptions and images of who I thought God to be. I've moved into experiencing God as the mysterious holy web that holds all, knows all, and is *in* all. This has helped me start to understand that every *thing* belongs, and that every *thing* is spiritual.

The transformative mystery of grace has changed me and healed me at the deepest levels of consciousness. When I give it space, and learn how to let things go, the beauty of transformation flourishes. It helps me to remember that what I have today, that I didn't have in my childhood, is *choice*. I now have choices of how I choose to live and look at life.

Knowing and *accepting* these are the cards that have been dealt to me, I now ask myself, what's the invitation? It's as if I have discovered the knowledge of holding the key to set my own self free. It's up to me to be willing to unmask, disrupt, and dismantle my previous ways of being in order to find equanimity. To answer my life's invitation of being anchored. Every storm is just an opportunity to sink my roots down deeper. To stand tall like the majestic big old oak tree that actually *needs* the wind in order to strengthen. I'm grateful to have found peace in knowing that in the midst of it all, I don't have to keep my pain alive in order to keep my truth alive. By choosing to welcome the wind instead of avoiding it, I can intentionally breathe so much deeper, fuller, and with the desire to grow far beyond that which once tried to claim me.

*I'm writing a new story now.*

## I Am Me

Dear Adoption,
My name was Baby Girl Ridgefort
The meaning is: Dweller of the Stronghold
Adoption tried to claim me
Relinquishing me forever to the unknown
Coloring my world dark with a primal wound

Society says, "you must feel grateful.
After all, weren't you deemed unlovable/unwanted?"
So, I wore the impossibly heavy cloak of denial of self
Exacerbated by my adoptive parents need to shred my
    spirit
In hopes of birthing their own creation
Me sitting at the family dark hardwood table
Dissociating/Fragmenting
But God gave me a tenacious spirit

One of resilience and perseverance
Enough to eventually find my ghost mother
And enough to prove I was born
Alas, no cosmic connection with my natural parents
    transpired
Soon a distraction was needed
Too much pain
Needed to numb the emotions
My addiction was practically my end
And then my end

Became my beautiful beginning
Slowly taking back my peace of mind
Slowly putting the pieces of my true self together
Little by little

Day by day
One step at a time
I now choose life
No longer allowing adoption, or anything else,
    define me
Or to deny me
**I Am Me**

— EMMA STEVENS
12/10/18

# ACKNOWLEDGMENTS

In order to write my story, I first had to recall and remember. This brought a lot of the painful past back into focus. For me this was necessary to be able to get to the other side and start living in a new way.

First, my gratitude to my counselor, Don, who was the best guide I could have had to lead me out of a very dark place. Knowing my attachment style, he gave me a safe, nurturing place to explore everything I've always so diligently stuffed inside for far too long. He encouraged and welcomed me to allow him to be my safe container and all without ever any judgement.

Through the practice of Eye Movement Desensitization and Reprocessing (EMDR), I was able to visualize how to write this book. It gave me the ideas, the memories, and the chance to rewire my brain to experience my past in a new way. I'm so thankful to my EMDR counselor, Joanna, who made this process so creative for me and a new way to express myself.

To all the supportive coaches, teachers, editors, and friends who have listened to me and encouraged me – I send my love and gratitude for helping me get this story out of me and onto paper.

And forever, my heart loves and cherishes my two adult children who have taught me the meaning and power of surrendering to love. And that nothing else really matters. I'm so grateful to know and honor the special individuals they are and are becoming. I see you both.

I'd also like to thank my parents. Love and forgiveness go hand-in-hand.

Love to my big brother who I'm saddened had to leave this world so soon. You are missed.

To all my fellow adoptees, who I support and echo with the same but different experiences. May the healing begin and set forth a new way of being.

Emma Stevens
September 2021

# ABOUT THE AUTHOR

Emma Stevens is a U.S. domestic adoptee from birth and has survived layers of trauma that have put her on multiple journeys. She developed the inner strength and courage to surmount the many struggles she faced. Her traumas were born from being an adoptee who struggled with being forced to wear an impossible mask of playing the part of the "good adopted child." Because being relinquished and adopted has colored her life, it's Emma's desire to be part of the movement that is dedicated to helping bring forth change to the way our world views the needs and support of adopted individuals. She believes strongly in adoptees finding their voice and discovering their truth to have a solid sense of self and to reclaim their identities. Through telling her story, Emma is dedicated to help redefine the narrative of adoption to include the entire complex truth.

This memoir is Emma Stevens' first book. She has an undergraduate degree in journalism and has completed Master's level course work in psychology, specializing in Marriage, Family, and Child counseling. She has two adult children and two cat children who she adores.

Email her at emmastevens99@yahoo.com.

Made in the USA
Coppell, TX
22 October 2021

64500532R00111